RABBI SHLOMO EINHORN

JUDAISM
ALIVE

Using the Torah
to Unlock Your Life's Potential

D1571461

gefen publishing house
JERUSALEM ◆ NEW YORK   Est. 1981

Cover Design: Robi Onei
Typesetting: Irit Nachum

ISBN: 978-965-229-652-8

2 4 6 8 9 7 5 3 1

Gefen Publishing House Ltd.
6 Hatzvi Street
Jerusalem 94386, Israel
972-2-538-0247
orders@gefenpublishing.com

Gefen Books
11 Edison Place
Springfield, NJ 07081
516-593-1234
orders@gefenpublishing.com

www.gefenpublishing.com

Printed in Israel

Send for our free catalog

Library of Congress Cataloging-in-Publication Data

Einhorn, Shlomo, author.
Judaism alive! : using the Torah to unlock your life's potential / Rabbi Shlomo Einhorn.
    pages cm
ISBN 978-965-229-652-8
1. Self-actualization (Psychology)—Religious aspects--Judaism.   2. Bible. Old
Testament—Criticism, interpretation, etc. I. Title.
BM729.S44E36 2015
296.7—dc23
                          2015019308

This book was inspired by my wife Shira.

Shira means music and music is alive.

You ensure that my Judaism is always alive.

In memory of Edith and Cantor Mark Fishof
In memory of Rivkah Klein

May the words of Torah of their grandchildren and great-
grandchildren be a merit to their illustrious memory.
David and Karen Fishof

In honor of our dear children
Racheli, Becky, Shoshana, and Ne'ima

May the Torah continue to be the source of your vitality,
and may you enjoy good health, happiness, *mazal*, *brachah*,
and *hatzlachah* in all areas of life until 120.
Helena and Steven Usdan

Contents

Preface

"*Liberté, égalité, fraternité.*" I was standing on Rue Clovis of Paris in the winter of 1991 just in front of the Pantheon, when suddenly I heard the growing chants of a mob pronouncing "*Liberté, égalité, fraternité*" (Liberty, equality, fraternity). This haunting phrase has its origins in the French Revolution of 1789. The mob was running toward the building and I noticed that they had guns in their hands. I decided to run back into the Pantheon even though that was where they were headed, because I didn't want to leave behind my family, who were still inside. The young militants gathered all of us tourists together into a small space. One French native led an attempt at a protest but that was immediately silenced with the thrust of a gun to her head leaving her on the ground unconscious. They quickly ushered us, without explanation, to a cramped dark room in the basement. Was there a basement in the Alamo? That we can answer another time.

All of us feared for our lives. While we were sitting in the dark there wasn't much we could do but wait for our next marching order. In the middle of that darkness I heard a young women whisper to her friend, "If I make it out of here, enough is enough, I'm going to start living." I consider that the day that I made a conscious decision to start living. Life is a world with many colors, experiences, and opportunities; what a shame it would be to let them all pass us by.

What does it mean to start living? What does it mean to live a full life? It means that every day is filled with a sense of purpose. It means that your every step is a mighty one because it moves you one position closer to your mission. Living means that every life experience is exactly that – a life experience. Every moment, easy or difficult, is a chance to get to know the most divine creation on this earth – yourself. Living means knowing that you are infused with a tremendous ability to better the lives of those around you. Living a full life is about accessing the life you dream of. As modern-day explorer Kim Dinan puts it, living a full life is about "living a life on fire."[1]

Before we get too far ahead of ourselves, let us acknowledge that the problem with committing to living a full life is that a path toward fulfillment can often lead to a series of frustrations and missteps. If I were, for example, under the impression that attaining mass wealth for money's sake is the key to fulfillment, it wouldn't take me long to figure out that I had made a big mistake. Dr. Evelyn Bromet, a professor of psychiatry at State University of New York at Stony Brook, interviewed eighty-nine thousand people in eighteen countries, from very poor places to the world's most developed economies. Her findings: people in wealthier countries are more likely to be depressed. Overall, 15 percent of people in the wealthy countries surveyed experience depression, compared to 11 percent in the low- and middle-income countries.[2]

On the other hand, if I were under the impression that sitting on the beach and sipping margaritas every day with no agenda in mind is the key to fulfillment, it also wouldn't take much time before I realized that I was heading down the wrong road. Such a life holds no purpose, no drive.

How do I chart my course?

According to the ancient kabbalistic text the *Zohar*, G-d looked into the Torah (Bible) and created the world.[3] The Torah is the blueprint for the world. If that is the case, then a fulfilling, vibrant, and colorful life must comport with that design. The Torah must be the most effective manual for empowering us to lead a life of meaning and achievement.

---

1   Kim Dinan, *Life on Fire: A Step-by-Step Guide to Living Your Dreams* (CreateSpace Independent Publishing Platform, 2013), 3.

2   Evelyn Bromet, "Cross-National Epidemiology of DSM-IV Major Depressive Episode," *BMC Medicine* 9 (July 26, 2011): 90, http://www.biomedcentral.com/1741-7015/9/90/.

3   *Zohar*, Terumah, 2:161a.

An ancient rabbinic teaching, *"Hafoch bo, v'hafoch bo, d'kula bo"* (flip it over and flip it over, for it is all there),[4] drives home the idea that everything we need for a better life has already been embedded in the Torah. I used the title *Judaism Alive!* for this book because I have always believed that the Torah is not an ancient document with some useful wisdom from a bygone era. No. The Jewish message embodied in the Torah is elastic, vibrant, electric, empowering. In one word: ALIVE. Every story, every technical grammatical nuance, every suggestion is invigorating. But not everybody receives the Torah in that dynamic way. You don't need to be special or to have worked on yourself for forty years to uncover the majesty of the greatest of all texts. You just need to be open to receiving its tender word. We need to slowly make of ourselves a *kli*, a powerful vessel able to receive life's wondrous messages.

This little book is replete with teachings from masters who have dedicated their lives to unleashing the power of the Torah's words. I have personally met many of these masters, and I have seen how they transform themselves into the ideal vessels to receive the Torah. I watched in awe as I saw Rav Yosef Shalom Elyashiv, a scholar with an enveloping white beard, study Torah with the vigor of one who has found the greatest treasure. He did this on one and a half hours of sleep a night! I listened in wonderment to the human encyclopedia Rav Ovadia Yosef recite passages and texts spanning hundreds of years as though he were merely recounting the names of his children. I experienced in fullness the kindness of Rebbetzin Batsheva Kanievsky who met with thousands of sick, needy, and depressed people who traveled from afar to hear her potent blessings.

These three special people of blessed memory live on in their legacy. There are many beautiful vessels out there who receive the Torah so completely and live to share its living, breathing message with us. Some of that is what I attempt to discover with you here.

In this book we will follow the wisdom of three biblical giants who stood up against the world, paved a new way, and found a life worth

---

4 Ethics of the Fathers 5.22.

living. The first section of this book adapts the courageous initiatives of Abraham as a point of departure for discovery and recovery. The second section of this book gleans from the visionary life of Joseph – who navigated tremendous hurdles because he had a powerful ability to dream and foretell – as a metaphor for charting a personal life path. The third section of this book harnesses the tenacious skill set of Moses as a symbol of how get to the top and stay there.

These teachings are not a destination; rather, they are the starting point for a greater journey. Use this book as a springboard for deeper discussion, thoughtful pushback, and nuanced self-exploration. Enjoy the journey.

Note: Your deeper knowledge of the Bible and its commentaries will only serve to enhance your discussion while reading this book, but limited knowledge of the Hebrew Bible will not be a hindrance. Every concept, character, and term is locally defined and accessible. Translations of biblical sources are the author's.

Acknowledgments

Thank you to G-d. This work is meaningless without You.

Thank you to my initial editor Einat Tubi.

Thank you to Kezia Raffel Pride and the entire team over at Gefen Publishing House for taking this work to its final product.

Thank you to my wonderful school and community at Yeshivat Yavneh, where many of these teachings were developed.

Thank you to the newspaper the *Jewish Home*, who continually force me to write more material like this.

Thank you to my parents and family, who encourage, praise, and constantly promote my work.

Thank you to my fabulous children, who give me a long-term reason to write.

And most of all thank you to Shira, my life's song.

PART 1

ABRAHAM

WHERE YOU'VE NEVER BEEN BEFORE – HOW TO UNCOVER NEW IDEAS

And G-d said to Abraham, You shall surely go... – Genesis 12:1

The more original a discovery, the more obvious it seems afterward. – Arthur Koestler, *The Act of Creation*

Witty Forbes pundit Daniel Freedman points out one of the true ironies of life: there may be nobody more trapped in this world than a man wiped out from his return from vacation. He has absolutely nobody to complain to. Those who are not as fortunate as he has been to take a vacation are simply not interested in hearing him rant about how tiring all the flying and unpacking and taxis and going through customs was. You have to suffer through that fatigue on your own.[1]

But let's stop for a second. Why do we keep taking vacations? The preparation is extensive, the costs are prohibitive, the family fighting can be frequent, and the return home can be…well, we aren't allowed to complain about that part. So why do we do it to ourselves?

---

1   Daniel Freedman, "Are Vacations Bad for You?" *Forbes*, August 19, 2010.

On a philosophical level, what is the function of a vacation? Escapism, by its nature, can't work. Dutch painter Johannes Vermeer used his artwork to escape his chaotic and dysfunctional life, only to find that in the moments when he stopped painting he would crash emotionally much harder than before he had his escape. The distraction was not helping. Phillip K. Dick in his haunting short story "We Can Remember It for You Wholesale" (later adapted into the film *Total Recall*), illustrates the catastrophic results of trying to escape.[2] Again, why do we do it?

The value of a vacation is in acknowledging that all of life is about moving to a place where you have never been before. If you are blessed to take some time away with your children and family, focus on taking your relationship as a parent, spouse, sibling, or cousin to a place where you as a family have never been before. That is vacation. I don't mean geographically; rather I mean experientially. Experiencing the people you care about in a different backdrop and a fresh context helps you define the sweep of your relationship.

With this definition, one doesn't have to travel far to see something fresh and new. You can take a vacation for a few moments even in your mind. Shift your consciousness to an area or realm that you haven't explored before.

The story is told that German community leader Rabbi Samson Raphael Hirsch, at the end of his life, announced his plans to visit the Swiss Alps. When asked why he was going through this effort, he responded that he didn't want to stand before G-d on judgment day and be asked, "Samson, why didn't you visit My Swiss Alps?" This story addresses the Jewish stance on asceticism: not only are we not enjoined from taking pleasure in the physicality of G-d's world, but we will be called to account for refraining from material pleasures that were permitted to us. However, I believe the essence of this story speaks to something else as well: the migratory nature of the human condition. We need to keep moving.

---

2   Philip K. Dick, *We Can Remember It for You Wholesale and Other Classic Stories* (New York: Citadel Press, 2002), 161.

The Lubavitcher Rebbe, Rabbi Menachem Mendel Schneerson, explains the biblical verse "*V'halachta b'drachav*" (And you shall walk in His ways; Deuteronomy 28:9) in this vein.[3] The verse is not so much about following G-d as it is about walking, or moving. The human being is implored to be a mover. Our job is to take the soul somewhere it has never been before.

Philosopher, rabbi, and medicine man Maimonides (Rabbi Moshe ben Maimon, or the Rambam) compiled a list of the 613 biblical commandments. In his list he left out the charge to follow G-d in His ways. Why? Using the thesis of the Lubavitcher Rebbe, we can explain that Maimonides left it out because it is not actually a commandment but an instruction for how to carry out all the other commandments. It tells us that when we do any mitzvah (commandment), it needs to take us to a place we weren't inhabiting before. If you are not moved after helping the poor with a meal, then something is deficient; you've missed a key component. A mitzvah by its nature must catapult you to a different station.

In the beginning of his great and mysterious journey, Abraham was told by G-d in Genesis 12:1, "*Lech lecha*," which is usually translated "go for yourself," but literally can be read as "*go to yourself*." Abraham, G-d seems to say, there is no greater journey you can take, no more undiscovered terra firma than the edges of your being. Find it – bring light there. Move around within yourself and let your physical journey serve as a metaphor for your spiritual, internal journey.

Movement. We are all moving. Some forward and some backward, but we are all moving. All of life's vistas afford us a different vantage point from which to view life and from which to view ourselves. The spirituality that I have cultivated standing at the Western Wall in Jerusalem is in some ways different from the spirituality that I have cultivated while looking at a sunset.

But why, you may ask, do I need to go to a place where I have never been before? The Torah teaches us "*v'chai bahem*" (and you should live

---

3   Menachem Mendel Schneerson, *Likutei Sichos* (New York: Kehot, 1972), 34:37–38.

by them).[4] The law, morality, our good deeds – all are meant to be alive. There is a certain vitality to loving others, for example, when love is shared beyond one's immediate space. The difference we can make in the world is magnified when we open up our sharing to people beyond our own small circles. The Chilean poet Pablo Neruda expresses this concept when he says, "To feel the affection that comes from those whom we do not know…widens out the boundaries of our being and unites all living things."[5] My Torah study is given a certain gravitas when I can take what I've learned and explain its relevance and profundity to new students and to people in different parts of the world.

This, however, is where I am unsure. I am unsure whether we give our deeds life by bringing them to new spaces, new mind frames, new landscapes – or the opposite. Maybe the idea is that we give our new spaces life by bringing the deed to them.

Kabbalah, the study of Jewish mysticism, explains that at the earliest stage of creation G-d's light was too strong to be contained, and it shattered the holy vessels in which it had been placed.[6] The shattered pieces of the vessels have been scattered to the farthest reaches of the world (and some say to the farthest reaches of our souls). The mitzvah, the observance of our faith in action, is the catalyst that brings these shattered vessels back together. And like troubadours we go from place to place, with our deeds in hand, locating the lost sparks.

Go. Go to bring light all over the world, go to bring light to your traveling partners, go to bring light to the morality that you live. And never forget, there is no more profound destination than the core of our identity.

---

4   Leviticus 18:5.

5   Pablo Neruda, "Childhood and Poetry," in *Neruda and Vallejo: Selected Poems*, ed. Robert Bly (Boston: Beacon Press, 1971), 13.

6   Chaim Vital, *Eitz Chaim* (Jerusalem, 1910), 50–53.

Applying "How to Uncover New Ideas"

I will *uncover new ideas* by making a commitment to take the following steps:

▶ When attempting to generate a new and more empowering approach to raising my children, running my business, or eliminating a vice, I will not be afraid to mix and match classic strategies to concoct a fresh and killer recipe.

▶ I will take time to think creatively by briefly switching my normal brainstorming location, site of prayer, or exercise spot.

To Shuckle or Not to Shuckle – How to Learn from Creation

Go…to a land which I will show you. – Genesis 12:1

The human body is the best picture of the human soul.
– Ludwig Wittgenstein, *Philosophical Investigations*

We'll often hear the pop psychology trope "return to yourself" or "find the real you." We even explored a variation of that previously when analyzing G-d's command to Abraham "*lech lecha*" (go to you). But what does that really mean? What does it mean to "return to yourself"?

Have you ever watched a devout Jew in prayer? Often such prayer is accompanied by a back-and-forth motion. To sway in this manner is called in Yiddish to "*shuckle*." When we pray, should we *shuckle* or should we not *shuckle*? Rav Moshe Feinstein recorded that he himself stood perfectly still.[7] He prayed this way because he remembered in his youth the way the Russian soldiers would stand in front of their commander and they wouldn't budge for hours; they would stand straight as a board. Rav Moshe reasoned to himself that if this is how

---

7   Moshe Feinstein, *Iggrot Moshe* 4:107.

an officer stands in front of his general, then certainly when we stand before G-d we should stand at attention. Rav Yisrael Meir Kagan, the Chafetz Chaim, explained why he did *shuckle*. Psalms 35:10 says, "All my bones should speak of You, G-d." How do our bones praise G-d? They pay homage to G-d through their movement during prayer.[8]

I'd like to develop this last idea that our bones sing G-d's praises. The personification of one's body in the service of the Creator is a recurring idea beneath the surface of the Torah tradition.

The 613 commandments of the Torah, according to kabbalistic and other ancient sources, are parallel to the limbs and sinews in our body. Why is a connection established between each mitzvah and the human body? What's the bigger idea?

On the holiday of Sukkos, we take in hand the four species, four plants mentioned in Leviticus 23:40. The Midrash teaches us that these four plants correspond to four distinct body parts: the mouth, the spine, the heart, and the eye.[9] Why, again, does the ancient tradition link ritual performance with body parts?

In a later discussion, we will talk about how the Tabernacle, the holy abode built for G-d in the Wilderness, is described in the Torah in terms that are frighteningly similar to body parts. Why the constant use of this physical imagery?

Perhaps the Torah is teaching us that so much of what we need to know, so much of what we each need in order to live the best life we can, has already been embedded in our design. This epiphany describes exactly what happened with Abraham. He was raised in a culture that looked up to the stars for answers, the sun, the moon, worshiping all of these symbols and assuming that all of the mysteries of life are going to be solved out there. It's precisely at this point that Abraham asks, "How do I know I'm going to have any children?" (Genesis 15:3). G-d says, "Step outside, forget about your stars" (Rashi, Genesis 15:5). We don't believe that the constellations can dictate our lives. The stars' alignment

---

8   Yisroel Meir Kagan, *Mishnah Berurah* 95:5, 7.

9   *Midrash Rabbah* 30:14.

may in some instances give us a clue to life's trajectory, but we are not bound by its reading. And for good reason; the keys to a successful life are placed within us, and that's why G-d and the sages keep referring back to the human body. Everything we need is right here. You are the best answer.

When Abraham is told "*lech lecha*" (go to you), he is really being told by G-d, "Abraham, you're a searcher. You've been searching all over the world, searching to find Me. Some people go to ashrams on top of a mountain and some people go to the end of the earth looking for spirituality. You want to find 'It'? The answers you need to live your best life, most of them, are inside of you."

Rav Bachya Ibn Pakuda, one of Judaism's most important philosophers, once wrote that "we must investigate how a human is born, how all of his limbs are put together, and the function of each limb."[10] Why? What is he – a doctor? Why is this relevant? As a religious philosopher, shouldn't his writings focus, as those of such authors always do, on a life of morality and Torah observance? Rav Bachya clarified that "[examining our bodies] is the way we come in contact with the divine image inside all of us." We are all looking for one more book, one more distinction or idea that is hopefully going to change the way we feel about ourselves or the world. At a certain point we need to just stop and understand the world G-d put inside of us.

The Talmud tells us that a child is taught the entire Torah in the womb, and as the child is coming into the world, an angel taps him or her over the mouth. As a result of that tap the baby forgets all of the prenatally studied Torah. Why would G-d give us this entire body of wisdom just to take it away? Rav Yisrael Salanter explains that the information doesn't simply vanish, it's just pushed deep within the subconscious. Our work in this world is to access the knowledge deep within us and bring it out. There's a spiritual déjà vu that comes with this concept. When we hear something life-altering, we often have an intuitive feeling that we've heard it before. Perhaps we have! This is the spiritual DNA embedded within us.

10   Bachya Ibn Pakuda, *Chovos Halevavos*, 26–27.

The whole world is suffused with the truth of G-d's greater wisdom. Maimonides writes, "What's the way to come to love G-d and fear G-d? When a person thinks about his actions and G-d's creations and sees the great wisdom, with no end, he begins to appreciate G-d."[11] Meaning, look at this world, at yourself, at what G-d has done: a baby. And you appreciate. That's how you find what it is you need to learn about this world. The beginning of the *Zohar* says that G-d opened up a Torah scroll and from that He created the world. What does that mean? This whole word is encrypted with the words of Torah. When the Baal Hatanya, Rav Shneur Zalman of Liadi, was on his deathbed, his students asked him what he was seeing now that he was in the process of transferring into the next world. As he was lying down looking up, he responded that where once he saw a beam on his ceiling, he now saw the Hebrew letters *kuf, vav, resh, heh* – spelling the word *kora*, translating to "beam." He was seeing what is really the metaphysical foundation of this entire world. The Hebrew letters stand as the basis, because G-d looked into the Torah and created the world.[12]

Now we are ready to turn totally inward. To make our point we will stay on the cellular level. Our very cells indicate that there is a higher purpose. Every cell in the body agrees to work for the welfare of the whole. Many times cells know that it's necessary to die in order for the body to continue to do what it needs to do. Skin cells, for example, will die by the thousands every hour to allow for the replenishment of the body, for the immunization against microbes to continue – that is the cell's function. What a powerful message our body is sending us. With a higher mission and calling, almost all difficulties are traversable.

I once was officiating a wedding in Aventura, Florida. I quoted a statement from *Pesikta d'Rebbe Kehana* (a classic collection of Israel-based teachings): "A person should make himself the captain of his ship."[13] A prominent leader of another faith walked over to me after the

---

11 Maimonides, *Mishnah Torah*, Yesodei Hatorah (Laws of the Foundations of Torah) 2:2.

12 Rav Yosef Green, *Sippurei Hatanya* (Jerusalem: HaTargum, 1992), 136.

13 *Leviticus Rabbah* 21:5.

chuppah and asked, "Isn't that statement hubris?" Is it? No. It's destiny calling upon us to seize the mission we have each been given and to stay the course without flinching.

The second message our cells teach us is the power of communication. Messenger molecules will race to the farthest outposts of the body to get a message across to the rest of the body. Communication is a cornerstone of Jewish ritual observance. G-d left so much of the Torah unspoken. For example, men wear *tefillin* (special boxes placed on the head and arm containing scriptural sources) when they pray. How do we know that these little boxes are supposed to be black? Another example: fasting on Yom Kippur. Where in the Bible is that mentioned? A lot is left unstated because the key to ritual observance is communication. Judaism can't be packaged in one book. No. It demands a dialogue between teacher and student that has been maintained for thousands of years. You can't simply google all of your questions; human connection is necessary.

Cells also teach us the lessons of flexibility and creativity. They adapt moment to moment. Liver cells can perform over fifty tasks in order to get something done. And they can regenerate – the most amazing thing.

Efficiency is another lesson learned from the building blocks of our bodies. The physics of cells dictate that they function with the smallest energy expenditure necessary. They are designed to be as efficient as possible.

Finally, as Deepak Chopra is fond of mentioning, cells embody immortality.[14] No, cells don't live forever, but they do reproduce to pass on their knowledge; when the cell dies, the next cell already knows what it's designed to do. It's like the monarch butterfly that starts its migration from Canada, heads all the way down to South America, and then back to its place of origin. The butterfly that returns is not the same one that left; rather it goes through three or four lifespans before its great-great-grandchild gets back. How did the last one know that it has a summer home back in Montreal? Who told the butterfly? That's the eternity that G-d puts in all of us. Even when we're no longer here, the message that

---

14   Deepak Chopra, "The Real Secret to Staying Healthy for Life (Part 1)," *Huffington Post*, July 30, 2012.

we leave behind remains – whatever we've done, the influence, whether for big or for small, perhaps one word we've said on behalf of somebody else, or some gift that we've given to another struggling soul. That message stays on afterwards.

There is an ancient rabbinic teaching that is usually hard for people to accept. The teaching is that the forefathers and foremothers kept the Torah before it was even given. How could they possibly know what G-d wanted of them before any commandment was delivered? It now makes sense. If these colossal figures like Abraham and Sarah or Jacob and Rachel were so in touch with their inner beings, with a high enough dose of clarity they were able to intuit what G-d wanted from them by looking at their own inner worlds and the spiritual DNA of the world around them.

What a mind-blowing concept. The divine nature of creation allows us to perceive much of what we need to know simply by listening. We're typically not attuned to those messages. In fact, we fight the message that the human body is telling us. It's screaming at us, and we ignore it. Abraham was told, "*Lech lecha*" (go to you). This wasn't a mission; this was a blessing. May you find the wisdom to look within and grasp all the distinctions that you need.

APPLYING "HOW TO LEARN FROM CREATION"

I will *learn from creation* by making a commitment to take the following steps:

▸ I will take time each day to be still for a few moments, perhaps while in prayer. I will let the inner voice within guide my thoughts.

▸ Before eating or before performing any repeated daily behavior, I will listen to my body, listen to G-d's voice in the universe, and ask, "Is this good for me?"

THE RESERVOIR OF WILLPOWER – HOW TO HARNESS THE INTANGIBLE DRIVERS OF SUCCESS

And his wife turned to looked behind her, and she became a
pillar of salt. – Genesis 19:26

Strength does not come from physical capacity. It comes from
an indomitable will. – Mahatma Gandhi, *All Men Are Brothers*

What separates people who have achieved greatness in their lives and
those who have not? Often that gap is attributable to invisible factors,
things that you can't exactly point to. We love thinking that we know
the cause. Historians can conveniently look after the fact and develop
five causes of the civil war. But do we really know? Life is much more
complex than that. Wars, innovations, and significant moments are
usually due to a combination of factors that happen to collide at the
same time, thus creating opportunities that normally wouldn't have
been available. Carl Jung explained this phenomenon with a concept he
called "synchronicity."[15]

---

15   Carl Jung, *Synchronicity: An Acausal Connecting Principle*, ed. R. F. C. Hull (Princeton,
     NJ: Princeton University Press, 2010).

Malcolm Gladwell speaks about the unusual opportunity Bill Gates had in 1968 when his private school raised what was then a large sum of money to buy a computer terminal for its computer club. This may have been the only middle school in the country that had such equipment (which was far from standard even at the college level in those days), and Gates benefited from thousands of hours of free practice working with it during the formative years of his life. If he had gone to a different school, or been born a few years earlier or later, he would never have become the Bill Gates we know, because he wouldn't have had access to the computer and he wouldn't have had those thousands of free hours of training, allowing him to hone his skills and figure things out.[16] Much of life is a collection of invisibles working in consonance.

I'd like to focus on some of those drivers that distinguish us and give us our strengths and abilities to get things done. Focusing on the unseen is critical to any sophisticated relationship with Judaism. G-d calls upon Abraham to go to a land that he knows is there but he cannot see. Abraham is very disturbed by his father's idols. Why do they bother him? This becomes clear when we realize that for Abraham, religion is not worshipped in the tangible. The physical can't be a deity; something that you can point to, that you can touch, can't be G-d. We know this to be true of love – love is not something you can point to. You can point to acts of love, to behaviors that increase love. But when you ask, "What is love?" there is nothing specifically to which you can point.

Let me adapt an ancient illustration. A samurai warrior goes to a Chassidic rabbi. The samurai says to the rabbi, "So, you think you're so wise? Tell me, then, where is the gate to heaven and where is the gate to hell?" The rabbi, calmly sitting there, says to the samurai, "You know, you're so worthless. You walk around with that sword thinking you're powerful. I'm sure anybody can finish you off." At those words of insolence, the samurai reaches into his belt and unsheathes his sword, raising it over the rabbi's head. The rabbi, with a glimmer in his eye, looks

---

16 Malcolm Gladwell, *Outliers: The Story of Success* (New York: Back Bay Books, 2011), 190.

up and says, "That's the gate to hell." The samurai lowers the sword and puts it back in its scabbard. The rabbi says, "That's the gate to heaven."

Some things are just intangible. The most intricate discourse could never explain them as well as the simplest demonstration.

As they're fleeing from Sodom, Lot's wife looks back and turns into a pillar of salt. Why? Presumably, one reason is that G-d was saying you're not supposed to see this, you're supposed to believe in something that you can't measure, something that is intangible. Stop looking back. Life is often about the things we can't see. Many times those are the most valuable. Teenagers are usually bothered by the fact that we're trying to serve a G-d we can't see. But the truth is we know that some of the greatest parts of life are things we can't see. Can we see gravity?

When Sarah dies, Abraham goes through a difficult negotiation over a piece of land where he can bury her. Why? What's he really fighting for? It's a great big world – why won't just any spot do? Why does he need this particular cave? Abraham is again struggling for something that he can't see. The greatness of a cave is hidden from the eye. The worth of it you cannot see. The mystical work the *Zohar* talks about how the normal eye looked into this cave and saw nothing. Abraham looked into the cave and saw something – he saw the whole universe opening up in that one spot.[17] And he buys this intangible spot for his wife Sarah, who's moving into a world that we can't see.

Historians point out that this is what distinguishes biblical Egypt. Egypt was very much a world of the physical, a world of labor, of the pyramid, of what you can build. That's why when an Egyptian leader died, he was buried with his treasures, because in the Egyptian conception your worth in the next world was the physical assets that you accumulated in this one. This was also the reason for mummifying an individual: to try to preserve the physical. The Jewish message to the world at that time was that there is limited value to the physical and it has a short shelf life. At some point we enter into the real world, which is the world of the intangible.

17   *Zohar* 1:127.

This is the singular focus of the Sabbath. Every day we operate through commerce and barter, exchange, purchasing, and activity. On the fully observed Sabbath there is no increase. Nothing is purchased, earned, or created. The day that unfolds is simply the day that is. And therefore it's a day when you appreciate the intangible elements. Are there physical pleasures on Shabbos? Of course. But the idea is that it's your day to use the physical world to appreciate that life is much more about the intangible than it is about the tangible.

Now we are ready to explore the intangible drivers of our lives.

What is it that allows us to contribute the most in our lives? What allows us to be most effective? At face value, it's a science. If I exercise for so many hours, I will be ready for the race coming up. If I go through the following courses in such and such school, I'll be able to get X degree and thereby I'll be able to do Y and Z. The science of achievement looks at a series or a collection of tangibles and quantifiables that I need to do in order to get me from point A to point B. Larry Bird used to sit in his backyard as a kid and shoot five hundred baskets a day – five hundred shots and no fewer.[18] So someone like him might have been awkwardly tall and lanky, but what made him great was just consistency: five hundred shots every single day. That's the science of achievement. To achieve things in life, you have to go through a certain amount of grunt work to attain technical skill.

But we need to look at a different side of the coin. We just looked at what allows us to be most effective. But what allows us to be most fulfilled? That's a totally different topic. The science of achievement is well covered – there are books and YouTube videos on that. You could research and find out what you need to do in order to become a great chef. But that has nothing to do with the science of fulfillment. The realm of fulfillment entails a totally different skill set; unfortunately we mesh the two together and then we wonder why achievement does not automatically equal fulfillment. Well, I just worked hard, I put this whole banquet together, it was very successful – how come I don't necessarily

---

18   Larry Bird, *Drive: The Story of My Life* (New York: Bantam, 1990), 5.

feel better afterwards? How come I don't feel fulfilled? It's a different system of measurement. What's the difference between somebody who's been given plenty of opportunities, schooling, and job offers, yet spent his days in and out of rehab, versus a lot of people we may know who did not have those opportunities, those same possibilities, yet live their lives in success?

Many of us would say that our lives are dictated by our past. As Tony Robbins puts it, "Most of society believes that biography is destiny."[19] You're destined to live it over and over. Past equals future. Well, it does if you choose to live there; if you hold on to your past and keep on living it, then it really does equal your future. Rav Chaim Shmuelevitz says in the fourth chapter of his work *Sichos Mussar* that we'll go so far as to design fictional stories about our lives just to allow us to continue to let the past dictate our dysfunctional trajectories. We'll tell ourselves, for example, that a particular negative pattern "worked" in a prior relationship, even though that is not the case. Our minds are capable of making up a whole number of narratives to avoid the point of the real one.

Our past does hold the key to whether we have fulfillment or not inasmuch as it's up to us to choose whether we are there or not. At the end of the Torah, G-d says, "I put in front of you life and death, blessing and curse; choose life."[20] G-d puts in front of us all possibilities, and we're asked to make decisions that affect the path of the life each one of us will have. Dr. Phil says a person's entire life is dictated by ten defining moments, seven critical choices, and five pivotal people.[21] I'm not so sure life works out that neatly but the point is well taken. Map it out and we get the screenplay of our entire life. It's our job to audit that information and keep the things we like and get rid of the things we don't like. Our decisions shape our individual destinies.

19   Tony Robbins, "Why We Do What We Do," TED Talk, Monterey, CA, February 1, 2006.

20   Deuteronomy 30:19.

21   Phil McGraw, *Self Matters: Creating Your Life from the Inside Out* (New York: Free Press, 2003), 17–18.

We can boil down the process of making a sound decision into three components based on three iconic biblical moments.

1. Focus: Esau and his soup. Esau is sitting in the forest with two options in front of him: keep my rightful birthright, or sell it and get some soup.[22] Esau used a very narrow window to make his decision: What's more important to me *right now*? When we make decisions, do we focus on present value or do we think about the impact ten, twenty, or forty years down the line?

One of the critical components to any decision that we make is what we choose to focus on. If something happens to me, is that a sign of the beginning of a new way of life or is that an indication that something is ending? It's all a matter of focus. You could look at the same situation from two different vantage points. Steve Jobs was given away by his parents. They literally left him on a doorstep. The average kid could look at that event and say, "I was abandoned." Steve Jobs looked at it and said to himself, "I was chosen." My new parents chose to have me.[23]

There's a story that is told from the teachings of the Baal Shem Tov. One hundred people are all trying to get to the palace of the king, which is encircled by seven walls. The first wall is made of ice. Thirty-five people bow out after attempting that first wall. The second wall is made of glue. Another twenty people quit after trying that wall. Each wall is progressively more difficult. Finally six individuals make it to the final wall, which is made of swords. Only one valiant soldier makes it over. The king greets the triumphant one and asks him, "How did you get through all seven walls?" The brave one answers, "Because I woke up one morning, I looked ahead and realized that there are no walls."

You see, there never were any walls. Each individual attempting to pass through imagined a wall standing in his way. They even went so far as to imagine these walls in full detail. Because that's the story we sometimes need to tell ourselves in order to explain our own shortcomings.

---

22   Genesis 25:34.

23   "Steve Jobs," *60 Minutes*, October 23, 2011.

Our focus, our outlook on the world changes the obstacles that stand in front of us.

2. Interpretation: the banner. The second ingredient in making a decision is one of interpretation. The Hebrew word for miracle is *nes*, meaning "banner." Why is a miracle called a *nes*? Nachmanides answers that a miracle holds up a banner of G-d's relevance to the world.[24] A miracle raises our awareness and compels us to ask ourselves, "What does this event mean to me?" It's up to us to choose our interpretation.

Dennis Prager speaks about a concept he calls Missing Tile Syndrome.[25] A person lies in bed looking at tiles in the ceiling. Ninety-nine of them are aligned perfectly, but one tile is missing. The person keeps staring at the broken tile, unable to get it out of his or her mind. Some of us just see the negative. Two people can look at the same event and read it in different ways.

3. Concretization: The Song at the Sea. The third element of a decision is understanding that there's no point in having a vision if you're not going to do anything about it. There are no spiritual events for the sake of spiritual events. If it doesn't make me better, then there's no relevance. If it doesn't get me to do something different in my life, then it's a wasted moment. As soon as the Israelites crossed the Red Sea, they broke out into song – "Az Yashir," The Song at the Sea. Why? Rav Levi Yitzchak Berditchever says that they had such a spiritual epiphany at that moment, but it could have been worthless if it hadn't been concretized.[26]

Not only do our decisions shape our own lives, but they can affect the lives of others. When we make good decisions, we have the power to change the history of the world for the better. Because one woman decided not to sit at the back of the bus, the American legacy has changed forever. Australian Nick Vujicic is an amazing individual. Born with a rare disorder called tetra-amelia syndrome, he has no limbs. Nick

---

24   Nachmanides, Exodus 17:16.
25   "The Missing Tile Syndrome," Prager University, 2014.
26   Levi Yitzchok of Berdichev, *Kedushas Levi*, Shemot 15:1.

travels around the world to speak to people who have a lot more and at times want to give up.[27] People like us. He uses his ability to get up with no limbs as an analogy for life. Nick, at some point in his life, made a decision that he was not going to spend his whole life sitting in the corner of a room. Today he is married and raising a family. The secret is in our decisions.

What drives us toward certain decisions? Rav Wolbe, citing the Vilna Gaon, says that *ratzon* (will) is a tremendous power.[28] It is driven by specific needs that every human seeks to have met. Understanding these needs is the key to understanding the root of conflict. Often discord and strife between people is a result of a lack of focus on each other's needs.

As the Israelites are fleeing from Egypt they become nervous. They begin to complain and suggest that they should go back. "Were there not enough graves in Egypt?" (Exodus 14:11). How could they even think about going back there? Didn't they remember what their lives had been like? I was once at a *shiva* speaking with the mourner about his family, who is still in Tehran. I asked him why his family stays in a country where Jews are hated. He explained that this is the mentality of people in Tehran. They may live now with wealth – they're doing well by and large – but they don't realize, as is so often the case when you're inside a situation, that they're being used as pawns against Israel. They don't understand that. And in a moment the government can take everything away, they can hit *delete* and everything they have will be gone.

So why do people choose that life? Because it's what they know. They have the illusion that it's certain and predictable. People want certainty. They want to know that they can be comfortable, that they can avoid pain. The same goes for the Israelites in Egypt. Why did they want to go back to Egypt? Life was a known quantity there. They woke up, they knew they had to build at 5 a.m. They went to bed at night at 10 p.m. The schedule was the same every single day. They knew where

---

27 "How Nick Vujicic Triumphed Against All Odds," http://www.oprah.com/oprahs-lifeclass/How-Nick-Vujicic-Triumphed-Against-All-Odds-Video.

28 Shlomo Wolbe, *Alei Shor*, 120–22.

they were going to be at all times. There was no freedom. There was no independence. But you know what? It was certain.

And how do we gain certainty? We gain an illusion of certainty in our lives by controlling someone, smoking something, doing something that is going to provide a predictable stimulus response, an instant feeling of comfort. We rely on the crutches that have been there for us in the past, believing that these coping mechanisms will always be there for us.

After the first primary need of certainty, the second primary need is almost contradictory: it's the need for variety, uncertainty, the element of surprise. This was the complaint of the Israelites concerning the *manna*. It could taste like whatever you wanted. But it was the same experience every day. So the very same people who wanted to go back to a certain life in Egypt craved variety again. "We remember the cucumbers and the vegetation and the watermelon, things looked different to us,"[29] they proclaimed. We all have an innate need for a sense of variety in our lives. It's why you can't see the same movie over and over. We'll always need to do something different, to go to different places, live different experiences.

The third basic human need is suggested by Rav Nathan Lopez Cardozo.[30] He wonders why there is a Jewish custom to dance with the Torah on the holiday of Simchas Torah. The message we seem to send is an odd one. We're dancing with the Torah as if to say, "Oh, thank G-d we have 613 laws." Would we ever dream of taking the Declaration of Independence and dancing along with the Bill of Rights and the Constitution? You don't dance with the Constitution, with the Magna Carta. The custom is to dance with the Torah because of what it says about us: G-d trusts us to keep it, and its charges mean that we are chosen for a special mission, and we are capable of fulfilling it all.

This brings us to our fourth need: the need to feel significant, special, and unique. A positive way to meet that need can be through more spirituality, more education, teaching ourselves something different, or

---

29   See Numbers 11:5.

30   Conversation with the author.

getting involved in an organization. Alternatively, we can meet that need in a negative way. What do we do if we have no education, no resources, nobody gives us a job – how do we feel significant? For some people, the answer is violence. If I pull a gun on somebody I can be the king.

Next is the need for connection and love – the most basic element. The Maharal says that connection and love is the core component to attending synagogue.[31] It's not so much about a place where we can be most devotional; rather the value of it is coming together. It's the feeling that we need a sense of connection. No man is an island. We need each other.

The last two needs embody in many ways what real fulfillment comes from. It's the sense that we're always growing. Growth is the message of *lech lecha*. Abraham is asked by G-d to find himself and, in that, become greater. Growth is also the message of the angels and Jacob that even after all those years in the house of Laban, after all those years in such an immoral environment, the Torah says that Jacob encounters angels. Why does it tell us that he runs into angels? The fact that Jacob dreamed of angels at the ladder before he got to the house of Lavan, after all those years studying in a spiritual enclave, is not surprising; of course he was dreaming of spiritual beings. What else was he was going to dream of? The more remarkable occurrence is that after he left the house of Lavan he was still dreaming of angels. He never stopped growing.

We also all need to contribute. Life is not just about *me*. We need to be able to *give* in some way. Decisions affect our fulfillment in life. How do we make decisions? Decisions are a product of what we choose to focus on and what it means to us. Those decisions are further driven by a series of needs that the human condition makes a part of each of us. To understand what goes into any given decision offers us the most sought-after gift – the source and sustainability of willpower. All the modern research is pointing in the direction of a limited reservoir of willpower within each of us. Now it's time to understand what's in that reservoir.

---

31   Yehudah Lowe, *Netzach Yisroel*, chapter 3.

Applying "How to Harness the Intangible Drivers of Success"

I will *harness the intangible drivers of success* by making a commitment to take the following steps:

▶ I will take charge and become proactive with my life. I will not let decisions just happen for me. I will begin the proactive process by making a few pointed choices today.

▶ Before making any major decision I will ask myself how the way I view the world will impact my choice.

▶ I will sit down with a pen and paper and figure out what are my top two needs. Once I have identified them I will be better equipped to understand the patterns that I keep repeating.

Movie Making at High Altitudes – How to Find the Answers from Within

And He said to Abraham, you shall surely know that your children will be strangers. – Genesis 15:13

I am the world. – Robin Gibb

Let us for a moment turn a little inward. "*Lech lecha*" (you should surely go). Those were G-d's first words to Abraham. According to the Torah, G-d asked Abraham to begin a journey to the land of Canaan. Rav Menachem Mendel Schneerson, the Lubavitcher Rebbe, beckons us to pay closer attention to the Hebrew. "Lech *lecha*." It literally means "go *to you.*" G-d didn't tell Abraham the name of the land He was sending him to. Ultimately the main purpose of the journey was for Abraham to find himself: "*lech lecha,*" dig deep within to uncover all the resources you need to build up what's eventually going to be called the people of Israel.[32]

---

32   Menachem Mendel Schneerson, *Likutei Sichos* 34:37–38.

G-d placed within us all of the tools we will ever need. Sometimes it takes others to help us become aware of the potential that lies within. This explains the Jewish emphasis on having a *chavrusa*, a learning partner, because we each can sharpen one another and bring out the skills that can go unnoticed. That's why it's good to have pushback from somebody else who can look us straight in the eye and tell us what's what.

Upon this great journey, Abraham has what we call in Kabbalah a *behirus hadaas*, a clarity of thought, of mind, a cosmic light of lucidity that suddenly turns on. In modern lingo we would call it a paradigm shift or an aha moment. It often can be a different way of looking at the same situation. And at times it's a way of rephrasing a problem or dilemma in our lives by shifting a perspective over a little bit and suddenly, voila, we have some new insight. That's the paradigm shift. Suddenly a light goes on.

We ask ourselves how we are supposed to make any major change in our lives. We've been stuck in the same patterns for so long. The ancient teachings refer to this with an analogy of a light going on in a room. Even though the room has been dark for forty years, the second the light goes on in the room, it's light. For there to be light in the room that's been dark for forty years doesn't take a whole lot of work; it just means that suddenly when that light is on, we can see. When we've been doing something for years, thinking a certain way, it's hard to get out of that mindset. It's definitely challenging. But once we come back to the core, to the unbiased self – suddenly we get that flash of inspiration, the *behirus hadaas*. It might not necessarily take years of work. It's about having the right vessels to receive the information we need.

The Bobover Rebbe says that this is why we start the Passover Seder with Kadesh (sanctification) and then Urchatz (washing hands).[33] Presumably it should be the opposite: we should cleanse ourselves first, and then we'll be ready for holiness. The Bobover Rebbe explains that we begin with sanctification before we cleanse ourselves because

---

33   Rebbe of Bobov, *Haggadah shel Pesach* (New York: Adas, 2004), 37.

sanctification allows us to elevate our faculties to a level where they can catch the frequency and comprehend the profound messages of the evening. In our prayers we ask that G-d *"taher libeinu,"* or "purify our hearts," because so many years of built-up spiritual plaque have stunted our ability to catch inspiration.

It was fourteen years ago and I was in Israel a week before Rosh Hashanah, the Jewish New Year. I was in a *makolet* (mini mart), and the cashier at the counter turned to me and asked if I had made a *cheshbon*, literally "an accounting." He was talking about the groceries – did I add it up? And I'm wondering why is he asking me this; isn't it his job to make the *cheshbon*? At that moment I thought to myself, it is before Rosh Hashanah and Yom Kippur, the Jewish days of judgment. This is my message: I need to make a *cheshbon*.

We always have to stay in a state that allows us to pick up the spiritual frequency. Judaism says you can never stop being teachable. There's no concept that you can't teach an old dog new tricks. The universe does not subscribe to that idea. The great teacher Rabbi Akiva (who only started learning at age forty) is the paradigmatic example. Abraham, Moses, and so many others grew and kept growing. They opened themselves up to new ideas and new paradigms.

Let's make this a bit more practical. We explored the concept of a *behirus hadaas*, a clarity of thought. Permitting our minds to open allows a flash of insight that suddenly changes the way we think about the way we live. A major shift in perspective waits right around the corner for us if we simply allow it. Here are a few simple shifts that can be made when we open ourselves up to new ideas:

1. Movie making. We all make movies. One way or another we are in the movie business. I bet you're wondering how come Hollywood hasn't sent you a paycheck. Allow me to clarify. At times we find ourselves to be unhappy or in a difficult space, but that is due to the fact that we are playing out scripts in our heads, whole scenarios that haven't even happened yet. And we build movies on top of the movies. "This person is going to say that, that person is going to say that." Or, "When she said that to me, this is what she meant." Sometimes we even repeat the film. We replay the event over and over and over again in our minds.

Movie making with our emotions can be very tricky. On one hand G-d gave us an amazing gift: the *koach hadimyon* (the power of imagination). That's what makes the human brain so impressive: the power to imagine. Let's say that we're setting up for a party. We can imagine what a particular table should look like and we move toward that direction. We imagine what a business is going to look like, so we build that business in that direction. It's a powerful tool. The Rambam says prophecy wouldn't be possible without the power of imagination. But we know that everything has a yin and a yang. Everything has a *sur me'ra* (distance yourself from evil) and an *aseh tov* (do good), a positive and a negative. The negative, the more challenging part of the power of imagination, is that we imagine a whole storyline going on in our lives that people must be thinking of us, or that because they're thinking it, that's what it must mean.

The Ishbitzer, one of the great Chassidic Rebbes, says that one of the most difficult enemies of the people of Israel as recorded in the Bible is the people of Midian. The Ishbitzer points out that moving around the letters of the word *Midian* gives us *dimyon* (imagination). Why? Because they were a group of people who knew that the way you attack is by playing with the imagination, enticing the opponent to create faux realities through the imagination.

Midian is a symbol of using the power of our imagination in a disempowering way. Contrast that with a method that uses imagination for growth. Rebbe Nachman of Breslov says that when our base desires are beckoning us, we envision a little person on our shoulders saying eat this, do that.[34] We make movies in our minds and we replay them over and over. Whether it was a negative experience or a traumatic event, the replay button is on auto pilot and we accentuate with embellishments, because we forgot the details of a story that took place so long ago. We simply replace the details with our own thoughts.

34 Rebbe Nachman of Breslov, *Likutei Moharan* 2:48.

A great quote from Eckhart Tolle, modern spiritualist and philosopher, explains that "the primary cause of your unhappiness is never the situation but your thoughts about it."[35] That's essentially what Rebbe Nachman of Breslov and the Ishbitzer are saying – it's the Midian effect, this power of *dimyon*, retelling ourselves a useless story.[36]

The award for self-help book with the greatest title may very well be Terry Cole-Whittaker's *What You Think of Me Is None of My Business*.[37] According to the Jewish tradition, a *shem tov* (a good name, i.e., having a good reputation) is something valuable but it can't define you. You can't let others' opinions of you write your story.

2. Accept and release. There is a great teaching in Ethics of the Fathers. A person must "*maker es mekomo*" (recognize his place).[38] What does it mean to recognize one's place? Often stress and pain are the result of an internal conflict between what should be and what really is. For example, you're driving in your car and you want to get to your kid's performance at school. At the same time you are stuck in a massive traffic jam. Suddenly panic and stress overtake you. Why? There are two realities competing in your mind. The reality of being stuck in traffic and the reality of making it to the production. These two realities are creating a clash in your mind which you are incapable right now of resolving, and that emotion when the two come at each other creates the tension, stress, agitation, and the resulting frustration.

The opposite happens when you recognize your place. G-d says this is your place right now. There is no other reality. Arriving to the production will either happen or it will not happen. But your reality is where you are right now, that's the space where G-d has me. "I am here, this is my place."

---

35 Eckhart Tolle, *A New Earth: Awakening to Your Life's Purpose* (New York: Plume, 2006), 76.

36 Mordechai Leiner, *Mei Hashiloach* (New York: HaMeor, 2004), 163–64.

37 Terry Cole-Whittaker, *What You Think of Me Is None of My Business* (New York: Jove Books, 1988).

38 Ethics of the Fathers 6:6.

If we wrap our minds around the present reality, then we're able to move forward with the stress negotiated. Maybe we will arrive at the school play, who knows? For now, we drive. Accept, then act. Whatever the present situation manifests, receive it as though you have chosen it. Judaism doesn't say we should live in the now and ignore future and past, but it does say that the bulk of our energy should be present-focused.

As the Mishnah in *Berachos* implies, in a future world of clarity we will acknowledge that there is only one real blessing for good and bad: "Blessed is the One Who is good and does good."[39] By accepting any given situation as is, we are better equipped to collect our energies and focus on what needs to be done.

3. Problems at higher altitudes. Problems seem to fall away with higher altitudes. The problem that a three-year-old faces – for example, he can't get the cabinets open – would not be a problem for us. The problem falls away when you elevate yourself to a higher level of consciousness. It becomes a baby problem. G-d tells Moses, Aaron, Joshua, literally all of the great ones, "I will be with you and I will stand with you."[40] What does that mean? Everyone thinks that means they're never going to fail, or there will never be a mistake, or a rebellion. They had all of those. These titanic figures had plenty of troubles. When G-d says I'm going to be with you, it doesn't mean you're not going to have setbacks and failures. It means something else much more empowering. *Since I am with you, and you know that I'm with you, you elevate yourself to a much higher level of consciousness. And those setbacks and problems, therefore, are really insignificant. They are not really problems.*

The reason we have kings in this world, according to the Talmud, is so that we can have a glimpse of what it means to have a King of all kings.[41] Now imagine if you had a meeting right now with a great king or a powerful president, and for some reason your shoelaces are not staying tied. That problem would be so insignificant to you because

39   Babylonian Talmud, *Berachos* 59b.
40   See for example Joshua 1:5.
41   Babylonian Talmud, *Berachos* 32b.

something so much bigger is going on right now: you're sitting in the room with the president at a small table in a private meeting with twelve people. It makes the fact that for some reason your shoes are not staying tied irrelevant. But if none of that were happening and you were just standing in the street and you couldn't keep your shoes tied, it would drive you crazy.

This is what G-d is telling His great leaders: "I'm with you," in the sense that "I'm elevating you to a higher level of consciousness." Not that I'm not going to let you fall and not that you're not going to have failures. But rather it means you can brush those failures off a little easier because you know you're playing a much bigger game. You're walking with G-d.

This idea is essentially embedded in Abraham's return to himself – it's his struggle to figure out how to reconcile his idolatrous past with his new path, how he's going to elevate a pagan mindset. How is a human raised in darkness going to improve the world? How is he going to be capable of *tikkun*, of repair? He looks to the stars, and he says to G-d, "I don't see anything coming from me. How do I know I'm going to have a destiny that's going to make a difference?" G-d takes him outside by the proverbial hand and says, "I'm going to make you more than those stars over there."[42] What was G-d showing him with the stars? Abraham looked around and saw a life of trouble, of struggle. Sometimes challenges. G-d says, you're not confined by the stars, you live above the stars, you live with a higher level of consciousness. When you see problems in front of you, know that they may be messages but they're not impossible obstacles. When you live at a higher level of consciousness, the problems fall away.

That's *behirus hadaas*, a clarity of mind. When we return to ourselves. When we explore within and examine the tools that G-d gave us, then we will find that there are powerful shifts of perspective waiting to be discovered.

42   Babylonian Talmud, *Shabbos* 156a.

Applying "How to Find the Answers Within"

I will *find the answers within* by making a commitment to take the following steps:

▶ I will stop and breathe. I will leave the phone on silent for a bit. These small changes will allow a *behirus hadaas,* a clarity of thought to stream through me.

▶ I will audit my internal belief system, looking at my beliefs about myself and beliefs about the way the world should work. I will figure out whether these beliefs are stories that I have told myself and in turn decide whether or not they are working for me.

▶ I will accept the moment as is, without judging it.

▶ I will try to take a higher altitude bird's-eye view of the world. I will study my life from a broader perspective. I will take time to notice the bigger thrust of my life. This will enable me to rise above my struggles.

JUST GET GOING – HOW TO BRING YOUR IDEAS TO LIFE WITH MINIMUM RESOURCES

And Abraham walked as G-d had spoken to him. – Genesis 12:4

Our souls are not hungry for fame, comfort, wealth, or power.
Our souls are hungry for meaning, for the sense that we have
figured out how to live so that our lives matter. – Harold
Kushner, *When All You've Ever Wanted Isn't Enough*

There was a time when aspiring music artists needed a record label and a lucrative contract for their songs to be heard. One hungry forward thinker named Derek Sivers changed the game. He created CDBABY. COM. CDBABY is a website that hosts independent artists and their music. Simple as that. This site turned into a huge success for Sivers and for hundreds of talented individuals waiting for that big break. When Sivers was asked how he got this almost-obvious concept off the ground, he didn't respond that he waited for hundreds of investors, or for record companies to notice him. He didn't wait for a full vision to emerge. He knew that he simply wanted to provide musicians a service, and that impulse was enough to know for now. In Judaism we would say that he "pulled a Nachson ben Aminadav." He jumped right in.

Rabbinic tradition teaches us that "*kol haschalos kashos*" (all beginnings are difficult).[43] The start of any project can be fraught with challenges, pitfalls, and fears. But the Nachshon knows that sometimes to get something done, you can't wait – you need to jump right in. Nachshon ben Aminadav was the brother-in-law of Aaron and military commander of the tribe of Judah. During the Exodus, the Israelites stood at the edge of the Red Sea. The water was simply not parting. Nachshon decided that he wasn't going to wait. When nobody else was willing to dare a first motion, Nachshon put his foot in the water and said, "I believe the water will split."

The Chassidic Rebbe of Alexander once interpreted an interesting Talmudic position in tractate *Sanhedrin* in a similar light.[44] The Talmud says, "*Kasha zivugin k'kriyas yam suf*" (finding a mate is as challenging as the splitting of the sea).[45] G-d is infinite – how can anything be challenging for Him? What is the point of this comparison? The Alexander Rebbe says "*kasha*" does not mean difficult, but rather, in Hebrew it can mean "a question" – the question that we may have when it comes to finding a life partner. Will I ever find him or her? How will I know that he or she is the one? These questions are similar to the questions at the sea: Will this water open for us? How will G-d save us with thousands of enemy combatants chasing us? The answer, at times, to these questions is *just jump in.*

A Nachshon beginning can be so powerful. We have a tradition that relates to the energy of the initial moment: "*Hakol holech achar harosh*" (everything follows after the beginning).[46] Why is that? Why must everything flow from the beginning? Because the beginning sets the tone. It says, "I am somebody who is willing to take chances; I am somebody who is going to do what Hashem needs me to do even if I am afraid." Once that first chasm is traversed, you are never the same.

---

43   *Midrash Mechilta,* Shemot 19.

44   Yerachmiel Yisroel Dancyger, *Yismach Yisroel* (Bnei Brak: Maggid Press, 1999), 167–68.

45   Babylonian Talmud, *Sotah* 2a.

46   *Pirkei d'Rebbe Eliezer* 42.

Malcolm Gladwell's favorite "tipping point" example is Roger Bannister's four-minute mile.[47] Once Bannister did the unthinkable in 1954 and ran a four-minute mile, he generated a tipping point which has allowed hundreds to break that same mark since. The record is currently seventeen seconds faster. I think this is more than a tipping point. This is about somebody believing that something never done before can in fact be accomplished. Jump in the water and resolution will follow.

Abraham was called Avraham Ha'Ivri. The commentaries explain that the name "Ivri" doesn't mean "the Hebrew," but rather "the one who stood on one side of the world against the other." Abraham was not afraid. He was not afraid that his way of looking at the world was different. He didn't give in to the thought that his burgeoning ideology flew in the face of so much history. No, with G-d's word, "lech lecha" – you shall surely go – Abraham understood that even with an unfinished worldview, not yet perfectly polished and clearly understood, he must begin his journey. His courageous Nachshon moment, when he left behind everything he had once known in pursuit of understanding a greater power in this world, changed humanity's destiny forever. *Everything follows after the beginning.*

Modern success formulas instruct us to develop a clear vision of what we want, create a plan of action, and then work through the process, tweaking changes if necessary along the way. But what if your vision is not yet fully formed, or the exact desired outcome is not yet known? Many times we don't know what exactly we want out of life until we've actually experienced it. While a grand vision is wonderful, you can't always wait for one to come. Sometimes you have to just get busy moving.

Stephen Covey in his *Seven Habits of Highly Effective People* advocates for starting with the end in mind.[48] Yes, that is effective. But Abraham did not know the end when he began. Joseph did not yet understand

---

47   Gladwell has cited this example in numerous interviews, although it actually does not appear in his book *The Tipping Point: How Little Things Can Make a Big Difference* (Boston: Little, Brown, 2000).

48   Stephen R. Covey, *The Seven Habits of Highly Effective People: Powerful Lessons in Personal Change*, 25th anniversary ed. (New York: Simon and Schuster, 2013), 102ff.

why with all of his vision he would wind up as a forgotten soul in Pharaoh's dungeon. Einstein did not initially know that E would equal mc². When he got turned on to physics and electromagnetism in 1895, Einstein saw that there were too many holes. He knew that our current understanding was wrong. How was he going to prove it? He wasn't sure but he got started, and dedicated the next ten years of his life to working toward a vision.

APPLYING "HOW TO BRING YOUR IDEAS TO LIFE WITH MINIMUM RESOURCES"

I will *bring my ideas to life with minimum resources* by making a commitment to take the following step:

▸ I will think about a project I have been pushing off, and start it… right now! I will think about a conversation I've been meaning to have with somebody, and have it…right now! I will not worry about it being imperfect.

THE WORLD IN A FACE – HOW TO LEARN FROM THE GREATS

My son, remember me always, and let the image of my
countenance be never absent from before your eyes.
– Nachmanides, letter to his son

When you have once seen the flow of happiness on the face of
a beloved person, you know that a man can have no vocation
but to awaken that light on the faces surrounding him.
– Albert Camus, *Notebooks, 1942–1951*

Rebbe Nachman of Breslov says that the first way to achieve authentic happiness is by seeing the face of a righteous person – the end-all message of our eternal quest for contentment! With everyone all over the world on a journey for eternal bliss, legendary philosophers locked out of this most elusive prize, and theologians lamenting existence without an answer, could it really just come down to hanging pictures of great sages on the walls of our houses? How can we understand the connection between looking at a face and our inner contentment?

The idea is not totally a foreign one to our tradition. There is a passage in Isaiah that states that "Your eyes should see your teachers."[49] The Talmud uses this verse to teach us a great mitzvah (law): on the holiday of Sukkos we do what we can to visit our mentors.[50] While it is very understandable to tell us to follow the ways of the righteous and upright, why should we be asked to watch them? What are we staring at?

Move back in history to the dark episode in the Torah where G-d is on the verge of destroying Sodom. Sodom was a city that was filled with iniquity to the point that G-d could not stand (so to speak) continuing its existence. Subsequent to G-d's report that He is going to destroy this depraved city, Abraham decides to pray to G-d on the people's behalf. His attempt to save Sodom is of no avail. G-d repeatedly turns Abraham down. Finally there is a shift and He appears to acquiesce. G-d says to him, "Fine, Abraham, I'll spare just one family; I'll save Lot and his relatives."

Lot and his family are given one instruction as they are leaving: do NOT look back at the destruction of the city, or else you will turn into a pillar of salt. The time arrives for Lot and his family to run out of the city. At the risk of utter destruction and the foreboding threat of disintegrating into a big pillar of salt, Lot's wife lets curiosity get the best of her and she turns around to sneak a peek at the town while it is being torn asunder. Remember, this was the one thing that she was absolutely forbidden to do. The Torah records, "His wife looked behind her and she turned into a pillar of salt."[51] After merely glimpsing the sight of the destruction, Lot's wife becomes rock salt.

Mrs. Lot's transformative demise can be labeled, to use the language of our sages, as a "nes b'toch nes" (a miracle within a miracle).[52] Not only was it a phenomenon that her body was chemically converted into a pillar of salt, but it was doubly miraculous that her body did so only after *observing*, from afar, destruction by salt in Sodom. If Lot's wife did

49   See Isaiah 30:20.
50   Jerusalem Talmud, *Eruvin* 5:1.
51   Genesis 19:26.
52   Babylonian Talmud, *Shabbat* 97a.

something wrong by not heeding G-d's word, why was she punished with the very same punishment as the people of Sodom?

Turn to the end of the Book of Genesis where the forefather Jacob is on his deathbed. Short of breath and ready to move into the next world, Jacob reaches out to bless his children. The Torah informs us that since his sight was diminishing, he had to bring his children close, and he had to embrace them and kiss them.[53]

The commentators note a problem with the text. What does Jacob's loss of sight have to do with the necessity to embrace his children? Why does the Torah teach us that since he couldn't see, he was forced to kiss his children? Secondly, is it critical, while we stand by and witness the last few moments of one of the most seminal figures in Jewish history, that we discuss the extent of his vision? The great Spanish biblical commentator Sforno[54] addresses this difficulty and develops an answer fundamental if only for its explanation of what a blessing is. When we give a blessing to another individual it means that we are basically handing over that which is the best of ourselves onto the other person. Jacob wanted to give his children his internal world, yet without seeing them, he could not fully bind his soul to theirs so that such blessing could be transferred. Instead, he quickly used an alternative means by which he could transmit the spiritual gifts that he intended for his children: blessing them *while* embracing them, hugging them, and kissing them.

What do womanly pillars of salt, our teachers' faces, and Jacob's physical grip on his children all have to do with each other? Let us quickly review our questions. First, why has it become a good deed on the holidays to visit rabbis? Second, why did Lot's wife receive such an unusual punishment from simply looking at Sodom? And last, why did Jacob ideally need vision to impart blessing to his children?

The answer to all of these questions sheds light on this perplexing path to achieving happiness. The Rebbe of Sochotchov, a nineteenth-century Chassidic leader known for his masterful teaching abilities, sets

53   Genesis 49:1.
54   Commenting on the above verse.

down a premise that changes the way we look at vision.[55] Colloquially, we understand vision to mean that when I, for example, stand at point A, and there is a tree in the distance at point B, I can see it but I am still here, and the tree continues to stay over there at point B. The Rebbe of Sochotchov says that this is not what mystical vision is all about. In our mystical teachings, when one looks at something, he or she is not merely gazing at that tree from afar, bearing no connection between here where we stand and the tree. Rather, viewing something assumes that in some sense while I see the tree that is over there, a part of me is mystically over there as well. My perception generates an intense connection with that which is being perceived.

With this we have a beautiful answer. Why did Lot's wife turn into a pillar of salt when she looked at Sodom, a place that was in the process of being turned into salt? According to our mystical definition of vision, when Lot's wife looked back, she was metaphysically really there in Sodom. So too, with this answer we can understand why we are told of Jacob's loss of vision. Through the power of vision, one can connect to something on a deeper level. Since Jacob was blind, he was unable to make this connection, therefore he had to compensate for it by physically embracing his children.

This fascinating idea can also help us understand the reason why we are taught to look at the faces of the righteous. A righteous person, in the most narrow definition, is someone who has, in a sense, come closer than most people to realizing his or her full potential. This doesn't mean that the great qualities that I see in another are far from me. Rather, the chasm that may separate us from the greatness witnessed in another can be rendered nil if we know how to look. When we look up to the people who are inspiring to us, this – in a mystical way – means that there is a part of them in us at that moment. Find your human inspiration. Whether the inspiration comes to us in the form of a friend we care about, a rabbi, or a teacher, it must be someone who has made full use of his or her G-d given tools.

55   Shmuel Bornstain, *Shem Mishmuel*, Vayeira.

For those of us who are not as mystically inclined, don't worry, there is also a more rationalistic way to understand the emotional benefit of looking at the face of a righteous person. A driving instructor once cautioned his young students that you always want to look ahead toward your destination and not let your gaze wander off to the side, because wherever your eyes focus, that's where you are heading. If you want to go toward righteousness, focus your eyes there.

Think too of what went through the mind of the early sixteenth-century Italian Renaissance artist Michelangelo as he was conjuring up his David. What did he do? What was his process? He had an unbelievably big chunk of stone that was completely unformed; yet he had the capacity to look at it and see tremendous potential. He was able to see the David.

This illustration can also explain the cryptic statement of Rebbe Nachman of Breslov. The idea is that when we look toward people who inspire us, people who have achieved such personal greatness, we stop and say to ourselves, look what someone can do with his whole potential. This individual was created exactly like each and every one of us. In many cases, he or she could have even been raised the same. Just like the chunk of stone that was formed by Michelangelo into a magnificent masterpiece, our lives can emerge as works of art from an unshaped beginning. We must realize that great things can happen for us if we have the foresight to envision a better life for ourselves.

This is one way to find happiness. We cling to people who are happy and who are good-natured. Why? Because it affects our lives. The brilliant and empathic twentieth-century scholar and sage Rabbi Shlomo Zalman Auerbach used to always smile. You would be hard pressed to find a picture of him without that famed beaming expression. He understood the impact that we have on each other and said, "Who am I to cause other people to be upset?" When we see other people smiling, it becomes contagious. Try living your life surrounded not only with sages and people with lofty dispositions, but also with people who make you feel more positive. When you look at someone who is filled with joy, that emotion affects you. If you frequently find yourself around bitter and sour people, it also directly influences you no matter what you do. We are not looking for perfection. Nobody is perfect; that's just part of the human condition. Rather, we are looking for people who constantly seek to work on their imperfections and come to terms with them.

On a mystical level, when we look, it means we are there. But on a psychological level, it makes sense as well. We look toward people who are unbelievable. We see pure inspiration in their faces; they teach us that we too can soar.

APPLYING "HOW TO LEARN FROM THE GREATS"

I will *learn from the greats* by making a commitment to take the following step:

▸ I will surround myself with impeccable role models. I will look to them for guidance and engage them with my questions. I will study the habits and traits of highly effective leaders, and seek to understand what sets them apart.

One Night in Tokyo – How to Stay on Fire

Who will ascend the Mountain of G-d, and who shall stay on
His holy place. - Psalms 24:3

It's against my religion not to double me. It upsets me. It
makes me think they're saying to themselves I don't have it
anymore. - Shaquille O'Neal

I remember, as a kid, my walk to synagogue February 12, 1990. That walk stands out because I passed a newspaper. On the front of the newspaper I saw something that I didn't expect to see. There he was lying on the floor out for the count. The undefeatable Iron Mike Tyson knocked out in Tokyo by an unknown named Buster Douglas. How could this happen? How could a 37-0 undisputed heavyweight champion of the world take such a fall to somebody who didn't have much success before or after that fateful night?

According to tradition Abraham faced ten critical tests in his life. The exact order is a matter of dispute. According to the most commonly accepted count, Abraham's tenth test was the test against which all are measured: the binding of Isaac. Abraham is asked to offer his beloved son on the altar and kill him. In the last moment G-d stops Abraham.

An array of creative thinkers have grappled with this scenario, from Maimonides to Soren Kierkegaard to Arcade Fire. The sheer magnitude of its implied tension makes it fitting for a tenth test.

But there is another way to count Abraham's ten tests. According to twelfth century Spanish scholar Rabbeinu Yonah, the binding of Isaac was the ninth test.[56] The tenth test was whether Abraham would find the most sacred burial plot for his deceased wife, Sarah. But what's the point of a minor league (although meaningful) test after he has already passed the test of the binding of Isaac? According to Rabbeinu Yonah's count, shouldn't G-d have stopped after nine?

I'd like to suggest two possible resolutions.

1. Zone of Proximal Development. Sometimes a great body of work can go largely ignored. A famous example of that is Galileo Galilei. This great sixteenth-century mathematician and scientist was considered to be beyond the pale and way too extreme in his lifetime. A large chunk of his theories went ignored until the world caught up to his brilliant mind.

Another example is Lev Vygotsky. He was admitted to Moscow State University in 1913 under a "Jewish lottery" that had a 3 percent quota on Jews. His work was considered controversial and non-applicable in the West for many years until a theory he developed caught our attention. His theory describes what he called the zone of proximal development (ZPD). At any given point in a child's development, some tasks are easy for that child and fall well within his range of competence. Some tasks are too hard, and the child will not be able to do them even with assistance. In between the tasks that are too easy and the tasks that are too hard lies the zone of proximal development, meaning the range of tasks that a child will be able to perform *with the assistance of a more knowledgeable guide*[57] This is a zone of potential stretching; with the right help, the child can learn a task and soon master it independently.

---

56   Rabbeinu Yonah Gerondi, Ethics of the Fathers 5:3.

57   Seth Chaiklin, "The Zone of Proximal Development in Vygotsky's Analysis of Learning and Instruction," in *Vygotsky's Educational Theory in Cultural Context*, ed. Alex Kozulin (Cambridge: Cambridge University Press, 2003), 40.

The ZPD theory posits that the area where a child is challenged – just above his current level of competence – is the sweet spot for child development. Information that is too easy is below the range of optimal development. Information that is too challenging is likewise beyond the normal mode of development. But if we can place a lesson in the perfect spot between too easy and too hard, then we have struck developmental gold.

The penultimate test of the binding of Isaac was simply too big. It was larger than life and therefore didn't truly assess Abraham's level. There are many people who step up to the plate when confronted with a massive, dramatic challenge, for example when tragedy befalls them. When the devastation is way beyond a manageable range, people may be very good at emerging at their best in those moments. But often, the response is less forthcoming when the tragedy or pain is at a more moderate level. We are less likely to go into "battle mode" when the situation isn't as dire. The same could be said for Abraham. Of course he stepped up at the binding of his son. It was such a huge test that it told us barely anything about who he really is. What is Abraham really like when the cause is not as dramatic? Finding a burial plot for his wife Sarah is deeply important for Abraham, but it is a natural part of life. How committed will he be and how far will he put himself out to secure one of the holiest spots in the universe? With this test, Abraham has found his zone of proximal development.

2. Iron Mike. I'd like to draw your attention, though, to a more important resolution to the question we posed at the outset. We asked why, according to Rabbeinu Yonah, there was a need for G-d to test Abraham after he passed the hardest of all tests – the Binding of Isaac.

Maybe the ninth test (the binding of Isaac) was simply too big. Allow me to explain. Without a doubt the greatest boxer of the 1980s was "Iron" Mike Tyson. Fights would end in record time as his legendary uppercut made a mockery of his opponents. But then it all changed with one fateful Shabbos night in Tokyo. The young legend faced the epitome of all underdogs, Buster Douglas. The world was shocked; Tyson lost.

What happened? Sometimes when you have done it all, you let your guard down.

Abraham had faced the greatest test that mankind would ever know of. He triumphantly stood up to the test and offered his son. But the real test only comes after you have achieved it all. Will Abraham have the fortitude to stay strong? Or will he let his guard down?

We say in Psalms "*mi ya'aleh b'Har Hashem?*" (who can *ascend* the mountain of G-d?), and subsequently "*mi yakum bi'mkom kodsho*" (who can *stay* in His holy abode?).[58] It's one thing to pass that great test. It's another thing to stay at that same level.

Our lives are an aggregate of peaks and valleys. We hope that there are more peaks than there are valleys. We need to keep in our minds that the goal is not the peak. The peak is just the beginning. When we reach the proverbial summit and accomplish a significant goal that we've been striving toward, it is at that moment that our real work begins.

The challenge with staying strong in your victory is that the weather isn't always the same. After an economic boom often comes an economic recession. After an innovative creative breakthrough comes a competitor who adopts a similar and sometimes more advanced strategy. How do we adopt the strategies that allow us to always stay winners?

There is a famous passage from the Talmud in which Rabban Gamliel, Rabbi Elazar ben Azaria, Rabbi Joshua, and Rabbi Akiva went up to Jerusalem.[59] When they reached Mount Scopus, they tore their garments. On the Temple Mount, they saw a fox emerging from the place of the Holy of Holies. The others started weeping; Rabbi Akiva laughed. They asked him, "Why are you laughing?" Rabbi Akiva responded, "Why are you weeping?" They said, "A place [so holy] that it is said of it, 'The stranger that approaches it will surely die,' and now foxes pass through it, and we shouldn't cry?" Rabbi Akiva came back to them and said, "That is why I laugh." The prophet Uriah, Rabbi Akiva told them, foresaw the destruction of Jerusalem. The prophet Zachariah foresaw

58   Psalms 24:3.
59   Babylonian Talmud, *Makkot* 24b.

its rebuilding. "As long as Uriah's prophecy had not been fulfilled," Rabbi Akiva explained, "I feared that Zechariah's prophecy might not be fulfilled either. But now that Uriah's prophecy has been fulfilled, it is certain that Zechariah's prophecy will be fulfilled." With these words they replied to him, "Akiva, you have consoled us! Akiva, you have consoled us!"

Embedded in this prophetic message of hope are the tools we need to keep our heads up.

1. Look ahead. Rabbi Akiva forecasted. The Mishnah in *Avos* says: "Who is wise? He who sees the *nolad* (result)." Or as Stephen Covey likes to put it: "Begin with the end in mind." A skilled manager is good at forecasting, seeing ahead. We can't simply live in a bubble ignoring writing waiting to be written upon the wall. Simulate results, predict possible pitfalls, anticipate movements, and plan accordingly.

2. Laugh. Rabbi Akiva was able to find the joy even in tragic circumstances. Different climates demand different approaches. Flexibility in the face of adversity creates the opportunities we need to flourish. My teacher, Rabbi Hershel Schachter, commented that great leaders need not ask what great leaders did in the past, but rather, what would such leaders do in this new circumstance? It's a profound nuance that changes the way we engage a changing global market. Taking our construct to a business model, for example, we might extrapolate that one should ramp up advertising during a recession. Why? During a recession most companies invariably pull back.

3. Change other people's paradigms. Rabbi Akiva didn't initially respond to his friends' question, "Why are you laughing?" Instead he retorted by asking them, "Why are you crying?" Why? He didn't just want to present his own view. He wanted to first shake up the way they viewed the world. In order to survive at the top or on an upswing, we have to be willing to shake up the culture around us. We have to be willing to make those who are part of our team or those who assist us in our journey open to a new way of viewing the world. We have to be committed to educating those around us toward the concept of flexibility, forecasting, and adaptation. This way, when change does come our way and circumstances are mercurial, we have a team in place ready to use a synergistic approach to staying atop that mountain.

May G-d give us the strength to climb the mountain and may G-d give us the ability to stay there in victory.

Applying "How to Stay on Fire"

I will *stay on fire* by making a commitment to take the following steps:

▶ I will identify goals in my life that are challenging yet not out of reach. I will volunteer to help others in a way that pushes me to be better. I will ensure that my goals are realistic and meaningful.

▶ I will practice the fine art of forecasting. I will try to predict results based on the data that I have at hand.

▶ I will learn to be flexible with my business and social interactions. I will not marry myself to the worldview that "this is who I am and that's it."

PART 2

JOSEPH

1956 AND THE BLINK OF AN EYE – HOW TO PREPARE FOR INSTANT SUCCESS

Then Pharaoh went and called Joseph, quickly, from out of the dungeon. – Genesis 41:14

Change can happen in an instant. – Tony Robbins, "Unleash the Power Within"

You might remember comedian Yakov Smirnoff. When he first came to the United States from Russia, he was not prepared for the incredible variety of instant products available in American grocery stores. He says, "On my first shopping trip, I saw powdered milk – you just add water, and you get milk. Then I saw powdered orange juice – you just add water, and you get orange juice. And then I saw baby powder, and I thought to myself, 'What a country!'"[60]

We always look for the quick solution. Time is money. Malcolm Gladwell in his book *Blink* argues that most of our decisions could successfully be made in a blink, or a split second. Gladwell claims that we have the ability to read people in practically no time. The message of *Blink* begins to get a little more muddled near the end, however, where Gladwell notes that some actions that take place in a blink are disastrous; for example, a police officer might shoot an innocent civilian because the decision to open fire was made too soon.[61]

So which is it? Should we expect change to come in a blink – or is proper protocol to wait our time and move at a more watchful pace? Well, like all good things in life, it depends.

The Chassidic teacher the Belzer Rebbe asks a thought-provoking question on the pre-Rosh Hashanah (Jewish New Year) prayer.[62] Somewhere around ten minutes before Rosh Hashanah, Jews around the world begin to pray the daily afternoon service called Minchah. The Minchah prayed immediately before Rosh Hashanah looks exactly the same as it does all year round. One recites the identical passages of nineteen blessings, which are said every day three times a day. One of the blessings that is said is *"baruch aleinu es Hashanah hazos"* (G-d bless this year). The Belzer Rebbe makes a daring suggestion; maybe we should remove that blessing from this final afternoon prayer of the year.

How can we ask G-d to bless this year when there are only seven minutes left of it (according to Jewish tradition, the calendric day begins at night)? What kind of blessed year is that? The Belzer Rebbe says something that will knock you off your feet in just four words: *Yeshuas Hashem k'heref ayin* (G-d saves in the blink of an eye). Wow! G-d doesn't need ten months to make it a year of blessing, G-d doesn't need eight weeks to change our lives, G-d doesn't even need four hours. G-d could change everything in the blink of an Eye. How rich is that vision.

My colleague and friend Rabbi Steven Pruzansky of Teaneck, New Jersey, wrote a fantastic article on what a hero is. He went through the life and times of Mickey Mantle. Whenever I think of Mickey Mantle I picture that 1956 baseball card with an innocent young rising star on the front. But his innocence ended there. There were those obvious warts

---

61   Malcolm Gladwell, *Blink: The Power of Thinking without Thinking* (New York: Back Bay Books, 2007).

62   Yissachar Dov Rokeach, *Peirush al Hatorah* (Jerusalem: Binyan Belz, 2003), 42–43.

like how he treated women, was initially cold to fans and media, was an absentee father… the list goes on. But what makes the Mick a believable human hero was the words he uttered in his last days as he was sick with cancer: "I'd like to say to kids out there, if you're looking for a role model, this is a role model. *Don't be like me.*"[63] That's an example of changing everything you've done and the trajectory of your life in the blink of an eye.

G-d can bring us our moment, G-d can bring us our chance to change so much of what we've done – in only a matter of seconds.

But let us go a little deeper. According to Jewish law, in the morning a man puts on his *tallis* (prayer shawl) and only afterwards the *tefillin*. This is the correct order because of the principle of *"maʾalin b'kodesh"*[64] – we move upwards in sanctity and not downwards, in a sort of spiritual evolution. Yet if the *tefillin* are in fact holier, shouldn't they come first based on another Talmudic principle, *"kol hamekudash m'chaveiro kodem es chaveiro"*[65] – that which is holier comes first?

One of the great minds of the twentieth century, Rav Isser Zalman Meltzer, solves the problem by stressing that there are two types of rituals – those that one performs which are external to the body (e.g., giving charity) and those that one performs with the body (e.g., *tallis* and *tefillin*). When it comes to rituals of the body, we follow the principle of *maʾalin b'kodesh* – we move upwards in sanctity. Why is this the case? Because when it comes to our personal evolution and progression, we must move step by step.[66]

When it comes to G-d, however, the Almighty could change everything in our world in a split second. Years of struggle and conflict, if G-d so chooses, can all be settled in five minutes. Years searching for the right partner in life could successfully come to an end by a chance encounter orchestrated by G-d. *Yeshuas Hashem k'heref ayin.* G-d saves

---

63   Steven Pruzansky, "Heroes," Rabbi Pruzansky's Blog, http://rabbipruzansky.com (accessed August 3, 2014).

64   Babylonian Talmud, *Tamid* 31a.

65   Babylonian Talmud, *Zevachim* 10b.

66   Isser Zalman Meltzer, *Har Tzvi*, Orech Chaim 1:20.

in the blink of an eye. But as Rav Isser Zalman Meltzer teaches us, when it comes to the work that we must do, we go step by step, brick by brick. G-d may work in the blink of an eye, but we don't. We must be deliberate. We must move with a strategy, a business plan, a charted course of action.

This dichotomy – that is to say, we move with a plan and G-d can make changes in the blink of an eye – is at the root of the Jewish historical experience. It's not our place, as humans in this world, to operate our lives expecting the miracle. That is up to G-d, not us. In truth, the real miracle is that we are given a mind, a strength, and an ability to summon a social army in the pursuit of a dream. To take a vision from start to finish and really see it through and watch a company grow – that is miraculous. To set goals for yourself that may seem slightly out of reach and work on yourself, step by step, until you find transformation – that is miraculous.

Plans, though, are a funny thing. As the Jewish proverb goes, "Man plans and G-d laughs." I think that statement is a bit dark for my taste. I would rather say, "Man plans, and sometimes G-d says, 'Stop for a moment what you're doing, and now look this way.'" Marketing guru Jason Fried in his fabulous book of pearls *Rework*, says sure, every start-up needs to design a detailed business plan, but be prepared at any moment to throw it away and shift courses if need be.[67]

I remember when I first became rabbi at a synagogue on the Upper West Side, my game plan was to avoid targeting young families. Hey, they're going to leave anyway in a year or two. After a year or two of my ignoring that demographic, G-d said, "Shlomo, your plan is great and all that, but you're looking the wrong way." I welcomed one or two young couples into our congregation and then came our blink of an eye. Everything changed in an instant. Within two short years we became the premiere synagogue for young families, perhaps in the entire tristate area.

---

67 Jason Fried and David Heinemeier Hansson, *Rework* (New York: Crown Business, 2010).

Make plans, follow that course, but know that at any moment – change can come flooding through.

Applying "How to Prepare for Instant Success"

I will *prepare for instant success* by making a commitment to take the following steps:

▸ I will find moments of stillness and calm. In those pristine moments I will harness the power of being deliberate and patient.

▸ While I am in the stillness, I will recognize that this generates an intense clarity and a tremendous potential to make a quick strike.

▸ When I learn to balance movement and stillness, I will practice making quick but thoughtful transitions in a snap.

FROZEN DREAMS – HOW TO TAKE ADVANTAGE OF OUR OWN STRENGTHS

So Joseph settled his father and his brothers in Egypt and gave them property in the best part of the land, the district of Rameses, as Pharaoh directed. – Genesis 47:11

I fly because it releases my mind from the tyranny of petty things; it gives me a sense of the wider horizons. – Antoine de Saint-Exupéry, in Richard Rumbold, *The Winged Life: A Portrait of Antoine de Saint-Exupéry*

Neuropsychologists call it "static state experience." SSE is a dream state where you feel as though everybody else is moving forward and you are frozen in your place. You can't call for help. You can't move your body. And you can't catch up to your group. Most people have a dream of that variation at least once in their lives. What does it mean?

SSE is labeled as a nightmare because the sensation that the people you know and love are moving forward while you are left behind is quite frightening. You are helpless and lost. Will you ever find your friends again?

Step deeper into the dream sequence for a moment. Let us analyze this experience. You are frozen but you want your friends to wait. Something else is bothering you here. You notice as they progress forward, they're smiling, even laughing. But how could they – you're not with them? They don't even seem to notice that anybody is gone from their group.

This dream is a projection of a fear that we all have. Others with whom we have shared so many experiences eventually may move on, find greater success and leave us behind as though we were never part of their lives. That is scary. The guy you spent every day of your childhood with – playing baseball, watching movies, sharing hopes – has now taken some corporate position on Wall Street. He hasn't called you in years. Or perhaps the daughter you raised settled down and found a great guy. They moved to Akron, Ohio, miles away from you, states away from you. She doesn't need you when she falls; she has him.

Our emotions are affected by many things. For some of us, it's the impact of our body language. For others, it's the syntax or words we use. But for all of us, what we choose to focus on directly manipulates our emotional state.

What makes this a nightmare is that we are consciously looking at our loved ones moving away. But this doesn't need to be a nightmare. Shift your perspective for a moment, close your eyes, see this dream and ignore those moving away. Instead, watch only yourself. What should bother you is not their movement, but only yours. Isolate your situation from the others.

You are frozen, but you want to move. When you separate out this frustration from the other fears, you are better able to deal with the task at hand. How do I unfreeze and progress? If you spend your time worrying about those moving ahead of you, you focus your energy on a process that you can't alter in a healthy way. If people you care about are destined to grow, if they are passionate about taking a position of great influence, you can't stand in their way. They're doing what they feel they need to do. You may try to sabotage, lay guilt, or buy into the idea that you're trying to protect them, but in the end you are still frozen in the same space.

Now back to you, the frozen you. Once you've isolated your situation from the rest of the image, you can now tackle your own challenge. New Age philosopher Eckhart Tolle in his book *A New Earth* uses the analogy of a person falling into a mud pit. If you spend your time worrying about how you could have been so stupid to fall in, or about what people would say when they see you in that position, you have neutralized your ability to deal with the situation. The past has happened already and the future is not relevant at this given point in time. All that matters is right now. Right now I am somebody stuck in the mud. This is the situation – accept it. Now, what can we do to emerge?[68]

Back to the dream. You are frozen. Don't ask yourself how you got here, or what life will be like without the others who have moved forward. Instead ask: How do I unfreeze? How do I find my unique voice? What can I do differently that I have not done before? What skill set can I learn that I have never learned before? And in the more difficult and trying circumstances, what beautiful memories and thoughts can I think of until G-d decides to send help or until G-d decides to reveal to me the power within that can solve my circumstance?

Gradually the ice begins to melt away. A whisper begins to emerge from your lips. You can feel your feet on the ground.

The Talmud teaches us the story of Rabbi Akiva.[69] Rabbi Akiva thought he was frozen. He thought that he had a soul that was impenetrable, a mind unteachable. Once, while shepherding his flocks, he gazed into a brook. He saw a hollowed-out rock resting under a gentle waterfall. He wondered how the rock, one of nature's hardest substances, had been hollowed out. When he was told that the water, over a long period of time, had made this hole in the rock, he reasoned as follows: "If a rock, so apparently impenetrable, can be hollowed out by water, how much more so can Torah study, which is compared to water, change my heart and mind?" He dedicated himself to learning Torah at the age of forty, and he became the great Rabbi Akiva. According to the Talmud, Moses

---

68   Tolle, *A New Earth.*

69   *Avos d'Rebbe Nosson* 6:2.

thought Rabbi Akiva was a greater man than he to give the Torah to the Israelites.

There was once a young scholar who went with his troubles to Rav Wolbe, a twentieth-century Jewish master ethicist and teacher. He said, "Rav Wolbe, I keep waiting for G-d to shine a light and let me know where I should go with my life, what I should do, but no light seems to come." Rav Wolbe responded, "G-d is shining a light on your path, but the problem is that you're busy looking at everybody else's path."[70] In the dream sequence, instead of focusing on our circumstances we are busy looking at everybody else.

Seeing the people you love move on is not easy. Seeing your former peers excel can also be challenging. But you know what? Certainly in the case of family and often in the case of friends, some value you possess or some vision you have shared has touched, ignited, inspired a reason for the people you love to grow and look for success in life. This means that a part of you is with them no matter where they are. When you can accept their achievements, swell with pride for them, and use those leaps as inspiration for your own circumstances, then you have truly turned a nightmare into a fantasy.

APPLYING "HOW TO TAKE ADVANTAGE OF OUR OWN STRENGTHS"

I will *take advantage of my own strengths* by making a commitment to take the following steps:

▸ I will accept and release my hold on the perspectives of those around me.

▸ I will learn to recognize when it is time to release my own previously held beliefs, and I will adjust my worldview as appropriate to my current situation.

▸ I will appreciate the movement and flow of everything in life. This will allow me to unencumber myself and get moving.

70   Heard from Rabbi Lawrence Kelemen.

THERE IS MAGIC EVERYWHERE – HOW TO MAKE THE MOST OF EVERY ENCOUNTER

And the captain of the guard charged Joseph to be with them.

– Genesis 40:4

It's so good to know that there's a little magic in the air. – Queen

None of us really know the struggles of other human beings. People who we assume live lives of perfection are often facing extraordinary adversity. This is not so much a variation of "the grass is always greener on the other side," but rather more about our obliviousness to the fact that there is "grass" on the other side at all.

Let me share with you a story about a student of mine. From your perspective he may seem to have it all, but the truth is, all that matters to our emotional state is our own perspective at a given time.

I was taking a walk with this student. Let's call him Ryan for now. He is a successful and good-looking doctor in his forties. He has every Jewish mother's dream – his own practice. One Saturday afternoon on the way to a class that I was giving, Ryan confessed: "Rabbi, my life has nothing. Every day I get to my office at the same time, I do the same procedures, my office staff does the billing – and that's it, every single day." It was clear that he had become a doctor to make a difference, yet now everything was all the same, day in and day out. No tension over whether this operation will work or not. No conflict with his office staff. No uncertainty as to whether he would be able to pay for the things he wants in his life.

We all crave certainty and stability in our lives, but we often don't realize that variety and – ironically – uncertainty can be tremendous passion drivers. Should Ryan tie one hand behind his back while doing a procedure? Should he hire off-the-wall office staff whom he can't rely on? I am sure that you would agree that this manufactured form of unpredictability is not the answer.

How do we make our often monotonous lives meaningful? Let's take a step back. For many people the humdrum of life is what they crave. Years of instability and a childhood of uncertainty could actually drive an individual to seek out a "boring" life. But for people like Dr. Ryan who crave the extraordinary, what should we do to generate excitement in our lives?

Malcolm Gladwell put together a collection of his essays in a book entitled *What the Dog Saw and Other Adventures*. The introduction to this compendium is inspiring. He digresses into a discussion about how he generated ideas for books and articles, and he asserts, "the trick to finding ideas is to convince yourself that everyone and everything has a story to tell."[71] Wow! Imagine living life with that mindset. Now, I don't like his choice of the word *trick* (and neither does he), but the essence is true. Everyone and everything has some story.

The founder of the Chassidic movement, the Baal Shem Tov, explains the Hebrew word *Torah* (Bible). Torah literally means "teaches."[72] The primary lesson, says the Baal Shem Tov, of the Creation story and the entire Bible is that anything that teaches is, at its core, Torah. If I learn about development from a butterfly, then that is Torah. If I learn about

---

71   Malcolm Gladwell, *What the Dog Saw and Other Adventures* (New York: Little, Brown and Company, 2009), 101.

72   Itamar Schwartz, *Bilvavi Mishkan Evneh: Peirush Baal Shem Tov al Hatorah*, introduction.

resilience from a disadvantaged child, then that is Torah. And if I learn about loyalty from my wife, then she is Torah.

Everyone has a story, everyone shares a lesson. Everything has a moment. The eccentric teacher Rebbe Nachman of Breslov encourages us to live our lives trying to find the inner wisdom of everything we encounter. I guess this is a deeper version of what Oprah means when she professes living mindfully.

Joseph was thrown into prison. He waited. For what? That he didn't yet know. But he knew deep down that there would be an encounter that would change his life. One day he found himself in prison with two new cellmates: a baker and a cupbearer. That encounter would provide Joseph with a pedigree only discovered years later.

At work or school, or anywhere in our personal lives, most of us crave a stable routine. Nevertheless, like Dr. Ryan, we want to feel alive. The opportunity for something new isn't far away in some mystical city on a cloudy mountain top. Every day, every step – and, yes, even every operation – brings us in touch with people and experiences that are new and diverse as the universe. Every store we pass on the way to work tells over a million new stories each and every day. Each of these stories is pregnant with the possibility of newness. Those stories contain the potency for innovation.

In 1801, Sir David Brewster graduated with an honorary master's degree from the University of Edinburgh. He was also ordained to preach. But his first sermon turned into his last sermon. Brewster was so nervous when he spoke that he promised never to preach again. In the words of a close friend of his, "It was a pity for the National Church of Scotland, but a good day for science." Brewster decided to pursue his first love, the science of optics. One day he broke a lens that he was working on, and all he had on him to replace it with was a piece of colored glass. Suddenly, a slight deviation in his day produced an invention that has captured the imagination of children ever since. Brewster called it a kaleidoscope.[73]

---

73   Mark Batterson, *Primal: A Quest for the Lost Soul of Christianity* (Colorado Springs, CO: Multnomah Books, 2009), 37.

Every passing moment is an opportunity to explore the endless narrative and nuance of the human condition. There is magic everywhere.

There is another direction in which to take this insight. We have talked about the fact that every moment and every interaction is an eye-opening opportunity. The opportunity is not just for us to feel alive, but also to make a difference in somebody else's life.

There are so many ways you can better other people's lives, and it can be so easy to do. A word of encouragement to a co-worker can entirely change his or her performance. A gesture of love to a peer can make insecurities melt away. Attending to someone else's needs can create an unmatchable rapport between two people.

Telling your children a story is the simplest, most innocent act in the world – but it literally shifts the course of history. Theologian G. K. Chesterton once said that fairy tales do not tell children that dragons exist. That, they already know. Rather, fairy tales tell children that *dragons can be killed.*[74]

What a world we live in. This is a world where every encounter is magical. Every encounter helps us align ourselves with destiny and choice. It's staggering: a properly placed smile, to the right person at the right time, can lift a soul and create a ripple effect that echoes throughout eternity.

Dr. Ryan, you are not just a doctor, you are a harbinger of magic and change.

There is an interesting but logical correlation. When we know that we are making a difference, we are also more productive. In a recent study it was found that telemarketers who felt that their work had an impact on people's lives actually made more successful calls. The key to your happiness at work is to understand the effect your work has on other people. Even if you are working on something as emotionally detached as welding gate wire, you have to use your broader vision to appreciate how the work that you do makes the world this much better. Every little gesture can have some greater impact. Seeing the importance

74 G. K. Chesterton, *Tremendous Trifles* (1909; repr., Auckland: Floating Press, 2011).

and magnitude of your small actions can make each day of your life a brilliant one.

APPLYING "HOW TO MAKE THE MOST OF EVERY ENCOUNTER"

I will *make the most of every encounter* by making a commitment to take the following steps:

▸ I will focus on something small or simple in my immediate orbit. It can be a doorknob or a table, a goldfish or a tent. I will look to identify its beauty and its contribution to the world. With enough clarity, I will begin to feel its true purpose.

▸ I will turn the camera inward. I will take stock of how I might have contributed to something, somebody, somewhere. When I identity that unique encounter, I will be better equipped to understand how I can give more and live aligned with my purpose.

Superman and a Wiki Page – How to Overcome Your Fear of Success

His (Joseph's) brothers said to him: "Will you reign over us?"
– Genesis 37:8

Black is beautiful. – Muhammad Ali

The Book of Esther is filled with revelry and jest. This light nature is not to be confused with frivolous behavior. In a sense, Purim – the holiday associated with the reading of this great book – is a serious joke.

There is a wonderful Chassidic tale that illustrates this idea.[75] Everybody in Poland knew about the most awesome Purim celebration in the town of Belz. One year, the Belzer Rebbe's pupil, Reb Yankele, showed up in the most perfect costume. He was dressed up like the czar of Russia. The likeness was so perfect that silence fell over the room as he walked in. The Belzer Rebbe turned to the "czar," who was really Reb Yankele, and in a commanding voice told him to remove anti-Semitic decree X, decree Y, decree Z. To all of them Reb Yankele said, "No problem. Consider it done." Then finally with a fire in his eye, the Belzer

---

75 Traditional folk story.

Rebbe said, "Remove the decree of the Cantonists." (This was the horrible edict that tore many young children away from their families to spend a solitary life dedicated to the Russian army.) With all seriousness, the Purim czar said no. The Belzer Rebbe screamed, but again he responded no. The next day when they all saw Reb Yankele, they asked him, "It was Purim – why didn't you just say yes?" Reb Yankele looked at them with blank eyes and said, "What are you talking about? I don't even remember being at the Rebbe's house."

While we may view the revelry and costumes as a cute way to engage the children in this holiday, there is an undercurrent in the Jewish tradition that views the camaraderie of Purim with tremendous profundity.

Let us develop this idea a bit further by posing two unrelated questions.

1. All superheroes have alter egos. In most instances there is a purpose to the superhero alter ego. For example, Batman uses Bruce Wayne to gain access to the hoi polloi of society. Anyone who has even a basic knowledge of superheroes knows that Superman's alter ego is Clark Kent. Why does Superman need the persona of Clark Kent? Superman is perfect in almost every way. Clark is a flawed, clumsy, awkward newspaper writer. There seems to be no ulterior motive in sustaining the identity of Clark Kent. Why keep this *schlemazel* around?

2. There is mystical link in that Yom Kippur is *Yom* (the day) *Ki-Purim* (*like* Purim). The names of the two holidays have similar etymological roots. The implication is that Yom Kippur is *like* Purim, but not exactly Purim. It sounds like it doesn't exactly reach the level of Purim. If Purim is in fact so holy, why do we spend much of the day horsing around and getting dressed up like clowns?

There is a story that the Chassidic rabbi the Gerrer Rebbe would tell every Purim.[76] A man goes to the Baal Shem Tov (the founder of the Chassidic movement) for a blessing on a certain pressing matter. The Baal Shem Tov tells him that he needs to go to a holy person named Reb

---

76   Shlomo Carlebach, with Susan Yael Mesinai, *Shlomo's Stories* (Jerusalem: Jason Aronson, 1994), 79.

Chaim Baruch. The only caveat is that this Reb Chaim is always drunk and therefore it's difficult to get him to give you a blessing. The wary blessing seeker heads over to the town where Reb Chaim Baruch lives. He asks the locals in the area where he can find this enigma. All fingers point to the local tavern. The man arrives there and sees Reb Chaim Baruch totally drunk. The *chassid* has a wild idea. Perhaps he can tie down Reb Chaim Baruch until he is sober. He carries out his plan by removing the liquor from Reb Chaim Baruch's hand, ties him down, and waits until he sobers up. At that point he receives his blessing!

Many days later, the man returns home and asks the Baal Shem Tov, why did G-d give such a power to a drunkard? The Baal Shem Tov answers that it is the other way around. This fellow is a holy person, who has so much light that it was too intense, too strong, and so he keeps himself inebriated. This, says the Gerrer Rebbe, is what Purim is all about. It is a day holier than Yom Kippur, but its light is so strong. The potential on this day for making great change in this world is so awesome, too awesome. Therefore, we mask this magnificence in a cloak of jest-filled play – costumes, drink, and an elaborate meal. But if we were to only realize the tremendous light of this day, who knows what we would be capable of?

Back to the case of Superman. The writer Marianne Williamson says it best: "Our deepest fear is not that we are inadequate. Our deepest fear is that we are powerful beyond measure. It is our light, not our darkness that most frightens us."[77]

Comic book writer Mark Waid makes the connection.[78] Superman is afraid of his power. He is afraid of his light. He questions whether his abilities will remove him from the community he wants to be a part of. Therefore, he hides behind the timid glasses of Clark Kent. We too carry

---

77   Marianne Williamson, *A Return to Love: Reflections on the Principles of a Course in Miracles* (New York: HarperOne, 1996), 190, © HarperOne. All rights reserved. Used by permission.

78   Mark Waid and Leinil Francis Yu, *Superman Birthright* (New York: DC Comics, 2004).

with us our insecurities about being too strong or too successful. And Williamson concludes:

> We ask ourselves, Who am I to be brilliant, gorgeous, talented, fabulous? Actually, who are you *not* to be? You are a child of G-d. Your playing small does not serve the world. There is nothing enlightened about shrinking so that other people will not feel insecure around you. We are all meant to shine, as children do. We were born to make manifest the glory of G-d that is within us. It is not just in some of us; it is in everyone and as we let our own light shine, we unconsciously give others permission to do the same. As we are liberated from our own fear, our presence automatically liberates others.[79]
>
> The questions we should be asking ourselves are: Do I realize my abilities? Do I know how powerful I can be? Do I fear my success? Here is an exercise that I think you will find quite powerful. Write your own Wikipedia entry. Don't necessarily post it online – you don't need to bare your soul to the world. But keep it for yourself. Write up your biography, your skills, what you're known for by others and by yourself. And then step back and ask the most difficult question: Knowing that this page is capturing me, could I be doing more for the world?

APPLYING "HOW TO OVERCOME YOUR FEAR OF SUCCESS"

I will *overcome my fear of success* by making a commitment to take the following steps:

▸ I will rise and grind, paying close attention to the G-d-given abilities with which I have been gifted.

▸ I will dig deep and become cognizant of the unique talent coding that runs through my blood. This intimate knowledge will inform all of my life decisions.

---

79   Williamson, *A Return to Love*, 190–91, © HarperOne. All rights reserved. Used by permission.

Captain Kirk and the Wife of Potiphar – How to Handle Our Turbulent Emotions

And she spoke to Joseph day after day but he refused to be
with her. – Genesis 39:10

Mercurial more wayward by the hour. The shackles fall away
I'm in your power. – Tim Rice, "The Fallen Priest"

We all would love to constantly live in an enlightened state. A state where nothing can hurt us and we only make good decisions. Read any self-help book you like yet sometimes there's simply nothing we can do with all the negative messages percolating in our heads. Follow all of the rules and still sometimes we can't shake the way we feel. The human condition doesn't allow us to retain the feeling of inspired majesty after watching a sunset. The question is, what do you do when you have the voice in your head, whether it's depression or anger? And I'm not talking about a chemical problem, some things are a chemical imbalance, or as the research shows, boil down to medicine. I'm talking about on a situational level. What is the Torah's view of how we deal with the emotional tempest that rages within each of us?

The rabbinic tradition explains negativity via the imagery of the *yetzer hara*, the "evil impulse." At the creation of the world, Adam and

Eve were warned to stay away from the tree of knowledge of good and bad. After they ignored G-d's charge and sinned – an impure impulse – the *yetzer hara* entered into their daily life. Yet if there was no dark impulse there to begin with, then how did they make this mistake of eating from the tree? And if there was always a darker force operating within them, what changed after the sin?

Rav Chaim Volozhin suggests a compelling resolution.[80] Once upon a time there was a snake, a cunning servant called the *yetzer hara*.This serpent came and calmly whispered persuasive dark thoughts into the ear of the human being: "Live a little, take from the tree." Once the serpent was able to corrupt Adam and Eve, the darkness of the *yetzer hara* was no longer an external beast whispering in our ears. It became something so much more devastating: an internal voice leading us away from our proper path. The philosopher Rav Eliyahu Dessler puts it pithily: "Before eating from the tree, *you* tried to get me to do the sin. After eating from the tree, it's *I* who want to sin."[81]

This was the shift that happened after Adam and Eve ate from the tree: the urge to do wrong went from being an external voice to an internal one. The gnawing darkness became a part of the process that we go through in our minds; it became internal and a component to our drives.

There's one more step here.

"*Ki seitzei la'milchamah al oyvecha*" (When you go out to war against your enemy)[82] The mystical tradition explains that this does not refer to a physical enemy on the battlefield; rather it refers to the internal *yetzer hara*. A shift happened in the world whereby our tendency to think negative thoughts, to go to a dark place, a dark mood, has crept inside of us and is no longer solely external. However, the key of this teaching – *when you wage war against your enemy* – is that it's still an enemy. It's not *you*. It's not you. What a powerful realization. We may

80   Chaim Ickovitz, *Nefesh Hachaim* 1:10.

81   *Haggadat HaRav Dessler* (Bnei Brak: Sifsei Chachamim Publishers, 2005), 71.

82   Deuteronomy 21:10.

have internalized an inclination toward chaos, but it's still not who we are. The negativity is not you.

There's nothing more integral or empowering to true growth than realizing that you are not the voice in your mind. There's a voice telling you, "Forget it. Don't do anything. It's useless. Don't volunteer. You're just going to complain and bicker." Or there's the voice that tells you, "Why would you go and help that man? He's probably just going to use that money to buy liquor." There's always a voice pulling us back, stunting our growth, giving us negativity. It's time to stand apart from that pull and realize that we are not the voice but rather we are the witness to that voice.

The moment you find yourself inching toward a disturbing thought, a negative and angry emotion, or a depressed sense of purpose, stand back and become the witness to that thought. Near the end of the Torah, in the portion called Ha'azinu, G-d beckons the heavens and the earth to bear witness to His law.[83] When Moses is no longer around, who if not nature will attest to the covenant made with the people? The biblical commentator *Ohr Hachaim* suggests an alternative understanding of "heaven" and "earth."[84] Heaven refers to those who stand high – the leaders, the innovators, the officers. Earth refers to the common individual. G-d was summoning humanity – from the people at the top to the people at the bottom – all to stand as the witnesses of the Torah.

The Midrash says that if not for the *yetzer hara* we would never build a house, get married, have children, or get a job.[85] What is the link between the presence of a baser impulse and our achievements? There is a famous *Star Trek* episode called "The Enemy Within."[86] Captain Kirk of the starship *Enterprise* is transported to another planet to engage an enemy combatant. As he is being transported, however, there is a glitch in the system and it splits him into two Kirks. Kirk number one is peaceful, loving, simple, and innocent. Kirk number two is tough,

---

83   Deuteronomy 32:1.

84   Chaim Ibn Attar, *Peirush al Hatorah*, Deuteronomy 32:1.

85   *Genesis Rabbah* 9:7.

86   *Star Trek: The Enemy Within*, directed by Leo Penn, Paramount, 1966.

mean, and vindictive. His loyal crew is trying to figure out which one is the Kirk that they should follow. They conclude that since they know Kirk is a good person, obviously they should follow the merciful and compassionate and kind one. At one point they have to make a decision, literally a fork in the road, but because this "good Kirk" is so soft and nice, he can't make the decision for them. He crumbles to the ground and starts to cry. They realize that while they had thought they had chosen to follow the better Kirk, in fact they had made a mistake.

The lesson here is that in order to properly function we need the totality of our human experience; we need to be the witness, to watch the full human experience and understand why G-d gave us that other impulse. Only someone who can get hurt is capable of being somebody who can properly love. This, perhaps, is why were given such permeating darkness. It's a gift.

When you have negative thoughts and emotions, instead of curling up into them and surrendering to the negativity, what you could be doing instead is witnessing, watching, or asking yourself, "What is this emotion asking me to do differently?" For example, when you feel anxiety about something, you can just get overwhelmed or you can stop and realize that the anxiety is sending you a message. Ask yourself: Why am I feeling anxiety? Perhaps you underprepared something and need to make a plan to get prepared. Or perhaps you simply need to wrap yourself around the fact that it's OK if you fail. That's what the message of anxiety is telling you: you need to respond differently so that you don't feel this way anymore. It's all a message. We become the witness, the one who is watching what is happening. That is the meaning of the teaching we noted above that if not for the *yetzer hara*, we never would have built a house, we never would get married, and we never would have children – because in order to build and accomplish, you need to have an impulse and a drive.

The Talmud says that the day the will to do idolatry was cosmically crushed, the nerve that helped us with prophecy was also obliterated.[87]

---

87   Babylonian Talmud, *Yoma* 69b.

What does one have to do with the other? This passage illustrates that even the darkest source has deep within it a holy spot. There is a purpose to the emotional turbulence that we experience in our lives.

Let us explore a second distinction. Anybody trained in marketing psychology knows that a strong salesman looks to create a certain level of pain for the prospective client; the close is achieved by showing how your product is the one to take that pain away. For example, an ad may show an elderly person holding his back, with a caption that reads: "Is your back pain killing you?" or "Are you having a tough time playing with your grandchildren?" Next comes the close: "Well, we have the *kayachupetz* comfypedic bed that's able to float in the air, and you'll never feel that pain again." That's marketing at its most extreme. We will do whatever we can to avoid pain in our lives, and this definitely drives our buying decisions. We'll pay a much higher monthly premium for faster internet services so that we don't have to wait for the answers.

Likewise, G-d gave us some great gifts to minimize pain. The Talmud says that a person should *yargiz* (anger) or encourage his good impulse to *fight* with his dark impulse, as it says, "Have trepidation and do not sin."[88] The Talmud continues and qualifies: "If you can win that way, great; if not, go and study Torah, for Torah is also a remedy." And in a final piece of advice: "If you can beat that dark side of yourself, great; if not, think of the day of your death."[89] Needless to say, this is a very strange passage. Can some sense be made of it? I think the key to this Talmudic source is to acknowledge that we mistranslated the opening line. We said that a person should "fight" with his or her dark impulse. That's incorrect. The Talmud never says that we should wage a battle.

Perhaps the opposite is true. On some level the message of fighting our dark impulse is futile and ineffective. *Yargiz* actually means "to excite." We know that trying to educate children through the modality of fear – yelling at them and telling them they're worthless, and if they do X, Y, or Z they'll suffer for the rest of their lives – that simply doesn't

88 Babylonian Talmud, *Berachos* 5a.
89 Ibid.

work. The *Saba of Kelm* pointed out many years ago what we know now – "hellfire" instruction died a long time ago; it stopped moving people. We don't fight the darker side in that way. We can't cut ourselves off. Judaism doesn't recognize the religious value of becoming a hermit.

There is a tradition that firstborn male children go through a ceremony called *pidyon haben* (redemption of the son) thirty days after they are born. The gist of the ceremony is that a firstborn child should by rights be dedicated to priestly service. The life of a priest, in the Temple era, could have been quite rigorous. In order for a parent to claim full rights back over their child, a *kohen* (one of priestly lineage) "sells" the baby back to the parent. The ceremony culminates with a major celebratory feast. Why do we make a party? On the contrary, the child was supposed to be dedicated to serving G-d in a rarified lifestyle in the service of a priestly family. Why are we celebrating the child's release from this service?

Rav Yaakov Kamenetsky tackles this problem and says that our ideal is not to live a separatist life divorced from the world. Our goal in this world is to transform the mundane, not escape it.[90]

Life is not meant to be avoided. The emotional torrents of our soul are not meant to be medicated away. On Passover, leavened bread – *chametz* – is viewed as a symbol of all that is bad in this world. It is puffed up, pretending to be more than it is. It draws us in, causing us to escape the realities of life. If *chametz* is so vilified on Passover, why is the *matzah* – unleavened bread – featured front and center as the main mitzvah of the night? Unleavened bread is simply moments away from becoming *chametz*. Shouldn't then the main mitzvah of the evening be a fruit or some other object that can't possibly become *chametz*? Speaking to our point, the Kozhnitzer Maggid says that our work on Passover night is not to run away; it's to live right there at the edge, with confidence and with the knowledge that you can thrive. You need not expel the shadow within. You just have to watch it. There is no battle that needs to be waged within yourself.[91]

90   Yaakov Kamenetsky, *Emet l'Yaakov* (Montreal: Hatikra, 1991), 89.

91   Israel Baumel, *Drush l'Pesach* (Los Angeles: self-published, 1989), 37–38.

There is, however, another way to view pain and emotional distress. Pain can be viewed as a lesson instructing you to do something different with your life. Joseph's brothers threw him in a pit. Nothing productive became of Joseph's brothers while he was gone. How come? Because they lived through the pain and darkness of their actions and spent their lives shackled by that very atrocity. Now look at Joseph. What does he make of his personal hell? Joseph only begins to live the moment he is thrown into the pit. That is, the minute Joseph is thrown into pain and trauma, he uses that as an opportunity to teach the rest of the world a lesson, to reshape the destiny of humanity.

He teaches us what it means to resist temptations in the episode with the seductive wife of Potiphar. He inspires us about what it means to have courage, to say no, to rise from a pit, to come out from below and share a message to the world, to lead, to save money, to be flexible, to adapt to your surroundings while retaining your identity. Joseph only begins to become the messenger the moment he goes through pain. The brothers allowed their pain to devour them. Joseph used his pain as an anchor with which to hone his talents, his mission, and his life's passion.

Let's apply this to a specific emotion – anger, for example. What is one supposed to do with anger? One approach to anger is release. A therapist may suggest that we take a pillow and beat the garbage out of it. Express our anger and scream it out. This is not the Torah method. Fighting our anger with more anger only teaches us to accentuate that emotion or *middah*. This goes back to what we said above: to *"yargiz"* our good side against our dark side doesn't mean to have them do battle, it means to excite the good over the bad. And what does that mean? The witness.

Rav Eliyahu Dessler, Rav Chaim Volozhin, and many great sages throughout the millennia understood that with anger, you're supposed to look at it, watch it like a baby, take care of it. Take care of the anger. The prohibition is to continue the anger. Feeling anger is an emotion. That's not the problem. That just comes at you. It's the dwelling upon the anger, fighting anger with more anger, that's the prohibition according to the Torah. Rav Dessler says that a person becomes angry only when he knows in the depths of his heart that he's wrong, and then uses his anger to cover his mistake. This is precisely why we should watch our anger, study it as a witness, because it's sending us a message. It's telling us that the reason we are feeling so angry is because something has touched a nerve inside of us – maybe guilt – and it's causing that emotion to come out.

This is the bottom line message. Do not look at your emotions as defining you, but rather as a part of you that you can stand outside of and deal with, and in that way come to a better, more powerful, higher place.

Applying "How to Handle Our Turbulent Emotions"

I will *handle my turbulent emotions* by making a commitment to take the following steps:

▸ I will stand apart from the voices pulling me back and realize that I am not the voice in my head but rather I am the witness to the voice.

▸ I will seek to identify the signals that my emotions are sending so that I can begin to answer what it is that I need to do differently.

▸ I will learn how to harness pain and understand its role in making me a warrior for good.

Sitting Alone at Breakfast – How to Stay Divinely Connected

The Lord was with Joseph and he prospered, and he lived in
the house of his Egyptian master. – Genesis 39:2

I dream my painting and then I paint my dream. – Vincent Van Gogh

Millions of dollars are poured into the study of the basic human quest to find serenity. For some it means to feel connected, plugged in, or experiencing an active relationship with G-d. On one hand, the problem can be phrased as emanating from G-d not revealing Himself to us. Many people feel that when they talk to G-d they're talking to an answering machine and that no one is really listening. This is a symptom of a deeper spiritual problem manifesting itself in the lack of a feeling of connection with G-d.

Israeli educator and teacher Tziporah Heller points to a religious fallacy inherent in this outlook. Every day we wake up, we breathe, we laugh, we run, we survive. Those very consistent and animating behaviors and emotions *are* G-d's revelation. We are living in G-d's world. Life is one big intricate and complicated miracle that is designed to sustain life and trigger creativity. Revelation happens in real time and at every turn of our heads. G-d is there to connect to because we interact with G-dliness all the time and with every moment.[92]

The great *rosh yeshiva* Rav Chaim Volozhin argues that conflicting perspectives are often at play in our misconceptions. The dominant theme of his masterpiece, *Nefesh Hachaim,* is the concept of *mitzido* as opposed to *mitzidenu,* G-d's vantage point vs. our vantage point. From our vantage point it sometimes seems as if there is no Divine Presence among us. But from the accurate G-d perspective, Hashem is ever present in everything we do. So the problem is not one of revelation but rather one of connection or relationship.[93]

How is it possible to have a relationship with an infinite G-d? Or to state it a bit more pithily, how do we know if we are truly connected?

1. We may never know. A famous pop song from 1985 has the lyrics "I say a prayer with every heartbeat…. How will I know if he really loves me?"[94] The argument would then go that we pray with as much *kavanah* as we can and hope that some connection has been established.

This existential *safek* (uncertainty) is an untenable religious position. No strong relationship can be forged or developed if we don't know whether we are in it or not.

2. I think, therefore I connect. There are two steps within G-d's commandments: there is the raw action and then there is the resulting connection triggered by that positive behavior. In Jewish law there is a concept referred to in the Talmud called "*machshava k'maaseh*" (thought is equivalent to action).[95] Why can a positive thought sometimes fill in for action? Because if the goal of a mitzvah is the resulting connection

92   Tziporah Heller and Sara Yoheved Rigler. *Battle Plans: How to Fight the Yetzer Hara According to Maharal, Ramchal, Chassidic and Mussar Masters* (New York: Shaar Press, 2009).

93   Rabbi Avraham Yaakov Finkel, trans., *Nefesh Hachaim: Rav Chaim of Volozhin's Classic Exploration of the Fundamentals of Jewish Belief* (New York: Judaica Press, 2009).

94   George Merrill, "How Will I Know," performed by Whitney Houston, © 1985 by Arista Records. All rights reserved. Used by permission.

95   Babylonian Talmud, *Zevachim* 13a.

to G-d, then the very fact that we can think about the mitzvah and think about doing good creates our connection point. The Dinnover Rebbe suggests such a concept in his philosophical classic, *Derech Pikudecha*.[96] Our relationship is apparent because G-d's law is on our minds.

We may still need a bit more than that, because how do we ascertain the level of our relationship to G-d in the moments when we are simply living and not doing a mitzvah? One could argue, however, that living appropriately is itself a mitzvah.

3. How are you feeling? Semi-mythical self-help guru Abraham Hicks argues that one who is feeling good will feel that way because G-d is flowing through that person. Conversely, when we don't feel great, it means that we've disconnected from our Source. Hicks calls this an Emotional Guidance System. Check in with how you are feeling, and that will tell you whether or not you are currently connected to G-d.

While there seems to be a strong component of this outlook that may resonate with us, it too has its limitations. Take for example, an annoying morning. What if you wake up tired, knock your head on the breakfast table, accidentally spill the milk and then rip your coat on the way out? Connected or not connected, you're probably not going to "feel" great.

An approach that works. We need something that ensures our constant connection, not just for a moment here or there. Rav Itamar Schwartz in his *Bilvavi Mishkan Evneh* asks: how come on Rosh Hashanah we switch our prayers to Avinu Malkeinu (our Father, our King) and move away from the relationship manifest in *Ani l'dodi v'dodi li* (I am to my beloved and my beloved is to me)?[97] Because Father and King relate to a permanent relationship, while the lover and the beloved is often of a more temporary nature. On Rosh Hashanah we ask G-d for a relationship that is deep and enduring.

---

96   Tzi Elimelech Shapira, *Derech Pikudecha* (Monsey, NY: Dinov, 2004), 6–7.

97   Itamar Schwartz, *Bilvavi Mishkan Evneh* (Jerusalem: Bilvavi Press, 2010), Rosh Hashanah, 38–39.

How do we make our relationship last? On Rosh Hashanah we blow the ram's horn. As Maimonides puts it, the blast of the shofar is there to awaken the sleepers from their slumber.[98] We are being beckoned to answer our calling. In other words, to plug in means to answer our life's calling.

To plug in means to *answer your call.*

The Satmar Rav says that when you enjoy a particular mitzvah, and always look for opportunities to fulfill that good deed, you know that you were born for that mitzvah.[99] The tribe of Levi was given the privilege of carrying the Ark in the wilderness. The primary responsibility went to Kehas. Why didn't this right go to the firstborn, Gershon? Because this was Kehas's calling. And when you find your calling, and you commit to it, there's an unshakable connection that is forged.

One of the first chief rabbis of Israel, Rav Yitzchak HaKohen Kook, said, "I was created because the time had arrived for me to fill a vacuum in the perfection of the real world. If I were to commit my efforts toward fulfilling the purpose of my creation, I would be considered 'worthy.'"[100]

Purpose. It is by living with purpose that we find our connection. When we don't answer the call, the reservoir of fluidity within us dries up.

In 1955, a doctor named Robert Butler painstakingly studied the health and longevity of people over the age of sixty-five. This study eventually became an obsession for Butler. He went on to publish his findings in a book called *Why Survive? Being Old in America.* He subsequently won the Pulitzer Prize for his book. Butler's research focused on individuals between the ages of sixty-five and ninety-two. One of the key discoveries that emerged from his research was a direct correlation between longevity, health, and a clearly defined purpose.

---

98   Maimonides, *Mishnah Torah*, Hilchot Teshuvah (Laws of Repentance) 2:2.

99   Yoel Teitelbaum, *Vayoel Moshe* (New York: Satmar Publishing, 1973), Naso, 321–22.

100 Avraham Yitzchok Kook, *Orot HaKodesh* (Jerusalem: Mosad HaRav Kook, 1989) 2:455, 210.

People who had a strong sense of mission simply woke up differently than those with shorter life spans.[101]

When we live our lives with purpose, then even the "down moments" are part of our greater connection. Education author George Burr Leonard in his book *Mastery* puts it this way: "Could all of us reclaim lost hours of our lives by making everything – the commonplace along with the extraordinary – a part of our practice?"[102] Our whole lives are part of our mission.

This goes one step further. When living a life with purpose it is not only the in-between moments that can be purposeful and filled with connection, but there is also meaning when we slip and tumble. The great *rosh yeshiva* Rav Yitzchak Hutner once lamented about the deleting of the human, day-to-day stories in the lives of great sages. In his own words: "Know my friend, the root of your soul [*your connection point – SE*] is not in the tranquility of your positive impulse [*when you feel good – SE*] but rather in the battle you rage with your darker self."[103] The fall is part of the ascent. Living purposely is a life of connection. It's experiencing your world with G-d.

Applying "How to Stay Divinely Connected"

I will *stay divinely connected* by making a commitment to take the following steps:

▸ I will hunt down the purpose of my creation, knowing that if I can live with purpose I will live with a stronger connection to G-d.

▸ I will use my knowledge of my purpose to help me in getting through the in-between moments.

▸ I will let my life's truth inform and infuse the times that I stumble.

101 Robert N. Butler, *Why Survive? Being Old in America* (Baltimore: Johns Hopkins University Press, 2002).

102 George Burr Leonard, *Mastery: The Keys to Success and Long-Term Fulfillment* (New York: Plume, 1992).

103 Isaac Hutner, *Pachad Yitzchak*, Letters 67–68.

PART 3

MOSES

How to Slip into Darkness – Riding the High Tides

And G-d said to Moses, "Come to Pharaoh." – Exodus 13:1

The profundity of darkness to which a person can plunge and still survive is aligned with the height to which he can aspire to reach. – Pliny the Elder, *Natural History*

Close your eyes and let us meditate for a moment:

Imagine that you are standing at the edge of a mountain top. The view is breathtaking and the air is pure. A cool breeze sweeps through, and for a moment you are in the most uplifting spot on earth. Then, by accident, you trip on a stray branch. You lose your footing. You slip and fall right off the edge. With the luckiest maneuver, you find a rock that sustains your hold onto the edge. Wow. For a few seconds you are safe. You look down. What a mistake. Down is dark, down is cloudy, down is unknown and never ending. You are trying with all of your might to keep your hold, but it's slipping and you know it. You dig your fingers into the cliff as best as possible but the future is inevitable. And there it goes – your last hold breaks and you fall…

We all slip into darkness. Some of us often lose our footing. And some of us may lose our footing infrequently, but when we do fall it takes us months to come back into the light. Some of us never think that we will fall but after years of broken relationships, unfulfilled promises, and bankrupt acceptances we realize that we may not have noticed the fall but we sure are in darkness.

For the purpose of our meditation, allow darkness to be a metaphor for whatever speaks to you – sadness, depression, addiction, sin, etc. The mystical sources teach us that there is a metaphysical reality to this place of darkness – in one iteration it is called *chalal hapanui* – the empty void. G-d, when creating the world, needed to make space for people to be and exist. In order for that to happen, G-d created pockets of emptiness – dark spots, black holes. These empty voids, due to their recessive nature, are places of tremendous impurity and apparent godlessness.

Perhaps our low moods and the mountain tops that we fall off of take us into this empty void. So much has been written on avoiding depression. We struggle so hard and long to keep holding on to the edge of the cliff. We fear falling because we know that the empty void potentially transforms us into someone unrecognizable.

Perhaps there is another way to deal with this fear.

Moses is the only known righteous individual to consciously enter into the empty void. He went there to confront Pharaoh, the epitome of darkness. Moses was initially reluctant but he could not refuse G-d. Moses, as future savior of the people, needed to enter the darkest realm, the void Joseph Conrad calls "the unseen presence of victorious corruption, the darkness of an impenetrable night."[104]

How was Moses able to enter the court of Pharaoh and come out alive? The Torah teaches us that G-d's command to Moses came in the form "*Bo el Paroh*," loosely translated, "Go to Pharaoh." The literal translation, however, is "Come to Pharaoh." Doesn't G-d mean "go"? Why then does He choose to say "come"? My son, Yisrael, shared the following insight: the lesson here is that G-d was telling Moses, you may

---

104 Joseph Conrad, *Heart of Darkness* (New York: Dover, 1990), 57.

in fact be entering a dark world, a world from which you may feel as though there is no coming out, a world where you might not even be able to recall existence outside of that world, but I want you to know, Moses, come, for I am there too. You are not alone. I stand with you, wherever you are. Come. I will walk with you.

The most fearful part of entering into a low mood or a state of depression – or just a plain old funk – is that we are without control, penetrating a state that is so lonely and so isolating. But know that in this *chalal hapanui* – this empty void – G-d is there too.

Sometimes we simply get derailed. There are mistakes we make over and over when those rough patches hit. Tim Irwin, who addresses the collapse of six major CEOs in his book *Derailed*, focuses on critical principles to stay on track.[105] Let's imagine how three of his principles apply to Moses's situation:

- Character trumps competence. Being authentic to who you are always works at the end of the day. Changing into something we're not, compromising ourselves, further complicates the derailment. At the critical moment when Moses saw an Egyptian taskmaster beating the Hebrew slave, he understood that he was not like the Egyptians. He was not really one of them.

- Arrogance is a huge derailer. Moses was able to stay strong and in a leadership position through every setback because the Torah identifies him as "the humblest of all human beings."[106]

- Lack of self-awareness. Not knowing our gifts, limitations, resources, or surrounding environment further exacerbates our slight turn off track. Moses is described as being "humbler than all people." He obviously understood the extent of his powerful position. How then did he retain his humility? Moses was aware of what he could and what he couldn't do. That is precisely what made him an effective leader.

---

105 Tim Irwin, *Derailed: Five Lessons Learned from Catastrophic Failures of Leadership* (Nashville: Thomas Nelson, 2009).

106 Numbers 12:3.

Back to our meditation:

> You are trying with all your might to keep your hold, but it's slipping and you know it. You dig your fingers into the cliff as best as possible but the future is inevitable. And there it goes – your last hold breaks and you fall. You fall and fall and fall, deeper into darkness. The eerie silence is deafening. But you pause for a moment, and you breathe. Breathe in and breathe out. And there it is, you can feel it. What you feel is remarkable. You are not alone. You are not in a place devoid of redemption. It can't be, because you feel the unflinching, unavoidable presence of G-d.

I know it seems lonely there. I know it seems that the state you are in is unbreakable, and maybe for now it is. But presence demands that for at least a moment we accept where we are, we acknowledge what it's doing and then breathe. Feel your space filling with divine energy.

These dark emotional states are not necessarily bad. In one classic Chassidic interpretation, the line in the Jewish Grace After Meals "*bakol mikol kol*" (G-d blessed us "with entirely everything") is meant to express that the entire landscape of emotions that pass through us has value. The highs in life cannot be experienced without the lows. The success cannot be cherished without the failure.

We are not faulted for slipping into low moods. Our test is how we choose to deal with them. Do we acknowledge that things we say or do in these states may have repercussions after we come back out to safe station? Do we acknowledge that the things we're saying and feeling while in these states are impaired by our circumstances? Life-changing decisions and public proclamations should be held to a minimum while we are experiencing the darkness. The empty void is a state of being. It is not a time for our colorful creativity. It is a time to hold. It is a time to pause. Grip on to G-d, tightly, and let the emotion swim right through you.

Applying "How to Properly Slip into Darkness"

I will *properly slip into darkness* by making a commitment to take the following steps:

▶ I will recognize that the most fearful part of entering into a low mood or a state of depression, without control, is the pervasive feeling of loneliness and isolation.

▶ I will acknowledge that this is the *chalal hapanui* – the empty void – and G-d is there too.

▶ I will submit to the focus and presence that demands that for at least a moment I accept where I am, acknowledge what it's doing, and then breathe.

▶ I will feel my space filling with divine energy.

Is the Cyclops in Your Cave?
How Simplicity Is the Most Dynamic Solution

And the man Moses was exceedingly humble. – Numbers 13:3

Stay hard, stay hungry, stay alive. – Bruce Springsteen, "This Hard Land"

Odysseus and his men accidentally stumble into the cave of the Cyclops Polyphemus, who is away for a brief while. The men help themselves to all the food they could want. They are ready to leave with enough time to get away but Odysseus makes a huge miscalculation and says, "Let's stay to meet these beasts." Odysseus wrongly imagines that Polyphemus was raised with the same sense of love for the Greek virtue of hospitality. But this is not the case. Polyphemus in a fit of rage closes up the cave with a giant boulder and proceeds to destroy Odysseus's men, smashing several of them against the wall. The remaining few are horrified.

Polyphemus feels that he can take a nap as those few left in his cave pose no threat. While he is asleep Odysseus realizes that he can't kill the Cyclops because nobody will be able to get them out of the cave.

When Polyphemus wakes (and after several outings), Odysseus gives the Cyclops some wine. Polyphemus says that for that gesture he will kill Odysseus last. Polyphemus asks Odysseus his name and he says, "My name is Nobody." Several drinks later, Polyphemus is good and drunk. Odysseus takes a heated poker and stabs him in the eye. The Cyclops screams to the other Cyclopes for help – they come to the front of his cave and ask, "What's happening in there?" The Cyclops responds in a scream, "Nobody is attacking, Nobody is attacking me." "Well," the other Cyclopes say, "if nobody is attacking you then it's better we leave." And they do. Odysseus and his men ultimately escape.[107]

What I take away from this story is that sometimes our best bet is to be Nobody. When faced with the trappings of an out-of-control ego, sometimes safety comes by being Nobody.

Let us clarify. Being nothing and negating our identity isn't a goal in life. It isn't a healthy way to carry ourselves day in and day out as we live outside of caves. Yet from time to time it helps to step back and acknowledge how small we really are. Sometimes it helps to just be simple.

Abraham is often remembered for his mantra, "*Anochi afar v'efer*" (I am but dust and ashes).[108] Moses tells G-d that "without my people I am nothing." Their greatness, their magnificent and clear sense of mission was not lost by acknowledging how close to nothingness they were. On the contrary, to live with such humility despite possessing so much talent only serves to enhance our character and our identity.

There is a Chassidic teaching that every person must live with a coin in each pocket: one that says "I am but dust and ashes" and another that says "the world was created for me."[109] Identity, vision, and drive don't need to conflict with a healthy dose of humble pie.

We often assume that with greater achievement comes greater pride, and with greater pride comes an inflated sense of self, dominating ego,

---

107 Homer, *The Odyssey*.

108 Genesis 18:27.

109 Martin Buber, *Tales of the Hasidim: Later Masters* (New York: Schocken, 1948), 249–50.

and then the beginning of our downfall. But it doesn't have to work like that. Moses is considered the humblest of all human beings. How is that possible – didn't he once, while standing atop the mountain looking down at the people, stop and say, "Not bad, all these people here just for me"? No. And here is why. Moses is the epitome of success. As *Time*'s senior religion editor David Van Biema puts it, Moses is a universal symbol of freedom, law, and leadership. He was sculpted by Michelangelo, painted by Rembrandt, eulogized by historian Elie Wiesel as "the most solitary and most powerful hero in biblical history.... After him, nothing else was the same again."[110]

Even baseball managers grow eloquent about Moses as a paragon. When recounting why Mets star Bobby Bonilla failed to inspire his teammates during his first stint with the team in the early 1990s, Frank Cashen explained, "He was supposed to lead us out of the wilderness, take us to the Red Sea and part the waters. It didn't work that way. He said he couldn't swim."[111]

As Moses grew in greatness, something happened. The closer we get to G-d, the more we actually realize our position in contrast to the Almighty. We are nothing. Yet, we are everything. If we believe that we are doing G-d's work in this world, whether as a rabbi, a carpenter, or a Wall Street trader, then with each success we move closer and closer to G-d. And as we step a bit closer, we realize how small we truly are. You are "but dust and ashes," and at the same time, the world was created for you.

Craving simplicity in life can at times be the sweetest thing. I remember on a family trip to Israel we went to the Western Wall. There is a custom to make your personal requests of G-d while standing at the wall. Some people pray for their health, some people pray for spiritual redemption, some people pray for direction. My son, Yisrael, who at the time was three, stood in front of the wall. I asked him, "Is there something you would like to ask G-d?" His answer was the simplest,

110 David Van Biema, "In Search of Moses," *Time*, December 14, 1998.

111 Murray Chass, "Mets Take a Big Step Back to the Future," *New York Times*, November 12, 1998.

yet most powerful prayer that I can remember hearing: "Hashem (G-d), can I please have a popsicle?" The prayer of a child, so simple yet so powerful.

When the Moses saga is first introduced, the Bible tells us that "there went a man from the house of Levi."[112] Why not just identify Moses' father, by name? The great German rabbi Samson Raphael Hirsch claims that the Bible wanted us to know that pretty soon Moses will work his marvel. He will become the titanic leader who is famous the world over. "But you should know," says G-d, "after all is said and done, Moses is simply a human being."[113] He's not G-d. Simplicity.

After all the miracles, plagues, and bending of nature, Pharaoh agrees to let the Israelites go from bondage. He says to go *"k'dvarchem"* (as per your words).[114] In the end, what might have ultimately moved Pharaoh was not the blood and the frogs and the vermin but rather the simple words "let my people go."

Kurt Vonnegut and Joseph Heller were once at a party at a billionaire's magnificent estate. Vonnegut turned to his friend Heller and exclaimed about the host's wealth. Heller responded that he had something even better: enough.[115] Rabbi Moshe Chaim Luzzato in his opening lines to a work on self-improvement says that "I come not to introduce anything new, but simply to remind you of truths already known."[116] Simplicity.

Be strong, be clear about who you are, and don't be ashamed in your pursuit of success. Nevertheless, remember to stay simple and humble. As Bruce Springsteen says, "stay hard, stay hungry, stay alive."

And from time to time revel in the spiritual simplicity of a question like "G-d, can I have a popsicle?"

112 Exodus 2:1.

113 Samson Raphael Hirsch, *Hirsch Commentary on the Torah*, 2d ed., ed. Isaac Levy (New York: Judaica Press, 1989).

114 Exodus 12:31.

115 Kurt Vonnegut, "Joe Heller," *New Yorker*, May 16, 2005, 38–43.

116 Moshe Chaim Luzzato, *Mesilas Yesharim*, introduction.

APPLYING "HOW SIMPLICITY IS THE MOST DYNAMIC SOLUTION"

I will make *simplicity my most dynamic solution* by making a commitment to take the following steps:

▶ I will acknowledge the powerful awareness that keeping things simple can be most effective.

▶ I will affirm and pay close attention to the moments when I crave simplicity.

▶ I will be strong and resolute about my pursuit of success but at the same time I will remember to stay simple and humble.

Objects in the Rear View Mirror May Appear Farther Than They Are – How to See the Bigger Picture

Then I shall remove My hand and you will see My back, but My face may not be seen. – Exodus 33:23

Whatever happens is the result of the whole tapestry of one's life and all the weavings of individual threads from one to another that create something. – Sandra Day O'Connor

At times in life we lose sight of how profound something may be. We get distracted by the external. The Torah recounts G-d's exchange with Moses: "Then I shall remove My hand and you will see My back, but My face may not be seen." This is how G-d makes known to Moses the limit of human vision. What exactly is the meaning of this verse? The Talmud compares this world to night. Imagine that you are driving a car at night on the highway in the middle of nowhere. There are no lights on the road and you are wondering why the road curves so much and in such odd ways. You assume that the individual who built this road was utterly incapable. Little do you know that were it to be day, you would notice that the area around the highway is filled with mountains, rivers, and numerous other natural obstacles. Therefore, the architect of this highway was actually quite ingenious. There is good reason for the road to constantly curve.

The message here is that sometimes in order to understand, we must see the entire picture. One more illustration which gets the same point across but in a subtly different way: Imagine peering into a doorway and noticing two people engaged in an aggressive struggle with knives. On impulse you run into the room and tackle the two individuals to the ground. Suddenly you hear in the near distance, "Cut! Cut!" As it turns out, you have just jumped onto a movie set. Many times we are missing an important piece of information when we fail to see the whole picture.

The Talmud speaks of a *bar yochni*,[117] a gigantic bird that with one drop of its egg can wipe out an entire city. What in the world does that mean? What kind of bird can do such a thing? Imagine, poses Rabbi Yisrael Salanter, father of the Jewish ethical movement, finding a newspaper clipping many years after its initial printing with the header on the article reading, "Drop of ink kills thousands." We would presume that we are reading about some preposterously lethal pen. But the truth is that in context, the headline is referring to a treaty that was signed, leading to the suffering of a group of people. Sometimes you need to consider the greater context in order to understand a seemingly isolated incident. Rabbi Salanter says that the same is true of the *bar yochni*.

This is also essentially what the holiday of Purim and the Book of Esther are all about. The miracle of their story is hidden within the text, and we are challenged to see the entire picture – to stand from afar and reveal the magnificent tapestry. The Talmud wonders where Esther is alluded to in the Bible. The Talmud turns to the words in Deuteronomy: "*V'anochi haster astir panai ba'yom hahu*" (But I will surely have concealed [*astir*] My face on that day).[118] Esther's name indicates what is hidden.

117 Babylonian Talmud, *Sukkah* 5b.
118 Deuteronomy 31:18.

According to Jewish law, there is a specific way to read the Book of Esther scroll. The reader unfolds the entire scroll before beginning because it is essential that we see the whole picture. Likewise, G-d's name seems to be totally absent from the Megillah because it is our job to lift up the curtain masking the real story.

Jewish tradition has both a Written Law (the Bible) and an Oral Law (the Talmud). The essence of the Oral Law is about revealing the hidden. It is there to reveal the message hidden within the Written Law. The Talmud presents the opinion of Rav Dimi Bar Chama, who says that G-d held Mount Sinai over the Israelites forcing them to accept the Torah. The Talmud then questions the legality of this acceptance, as it was against their will. The answer to the challenge is based upon a verse in Esther (9:13): "They kept and received," which teaches us that the people reaffirmed their commitment to the Torah, thereby asserting their voluntary acceptance in the days of Esther.

Why would they need to reaffirm their commitment if the Israelites already declared at Sinai, "We will do and we will hear"?[119] An ancient source called the Midrash posits that they voluntarily accepted the Written Law at Sinai but not the Oral Law. The acceptance of the Oral Law was affirmed in the days of Esther. Based upon our thesis, we can say that the reaffirmation was an expression that the holiday of Purim is a time when we have to bring G-d out from the hidden domain. It is a day that focuses on seeing the entire picture. This is why they accepted fully the Oral Law on this day, for that is the nature of the Oral Law – taking the commandments in the Torah and revealing their true detailed makeup.

It is critical that we begin to see the full picture, for without it everything in life seems so disjointed and distant. This is precisely our relationship with G-d. It seems to be hidden. We at times feel that we are so far from G-d. But were we to understand the greater scheme, we would see how close to Him we actually are.

119 Exodus 24:7.

There is a tradition on Purim to celebrate and drink a bit. Some explain that the state we bring ourselves to is *"ad d'lo yada"* (until he does not know), until the point where we no longer have clarity.[120] Why? Up until now we had thought that we are so far from G-d, but when our minds are in this semi-altered state we begin to realize that it is through this distance that we can come close. The perspective of near and far becomes blurred. When we lose our inhibitions, we no longer fear the distance. This is the reason for the extreme level of jubilation on Purim, for it is the celebration of an individual who was once so distant and now comes close. This generates the most intense joy.

The feeling of distance and detachment is, more often than not, a foible of our limited vision. We tend to see with tunnel vision and ignore G-d's hand in our daily lives. Every breath, every movement, every passing step is a miracle. Life's many tender dances are all signs that we stand right next to G-d.

I close with the words of country singer George Strait:

Just walked down the street to the coffee shop
Had to take a break
I've been by her side for eighteen hours straight
Saw a flower growing in the middle of the sidewalk
Pushing up through the concrete
Like it was planted right there for me to see
The flashing lights
The honking horns
All seem to fade away
But in the shadow of the hospital
At 5:08
I saw G-d today.[121]

120   Babylonian Talmud, *Megillah* 7b.

121   Rodney Clawson, "I Saw God Today," performed by George Strait, © 2008 by MCA
      Nashville. All rights reserved. Used by permission.

APPLYING "HOW TO SEE THE BIGGER PICTURE"

I will *see the bigger picture* by making a commitment to take the following steps:

▸ I will stand aligned with the awareness that while I may feel far from G-d, in truth a proper perspective will help me see how close I truly am.

▸ I will look at the world around me and appreciate that when I listen closely, I can hear the footsteps of G-d right by my side.

TO THE EDGE OF OUR UNIVERSE – HOW TO KNOW WHEN TO WALK AWAY

Because you [Moses and Aaron] did not believe in Me...you will
not bring this assembly into the Land. – Numbers 2:12

Know your limits, Master Wayne. – Alfred Pennyworth,
The Dark Knight

It was just after midnight as I stood at the bottom of a parking garage
in Secaucus, New Jersey. Over twelve hundred other people and I were
getting ready to walk through fire. For over thirteen hours we'd been
pumped with the message that anything is possible – and now we were
going to prove it. Flash forward two hours. I'm driving alone in my car,
totally lost somewhere near the Meadowlands – or is it East Brunswick?
I keep telling myself "anything is possible" – and then I tell myself, "Yeah,
so is getting lost."

The modern self-help movement, or millionaire messenger troop,
will tell you that we can do anything once we unleash the Kraken within.
Tony Robbins qualifies that statement with something a bit more
inspiring: what we thought were our limitations are not our limitations.
There is great truth to this paradigm. We all put up walls. These walls of

limitation are synthetic, creations of our own need for self-sabotage and, conversely, self-preservation. Nevertheless, at some point, you can fire yourself up – you can dig deeper than you've ever been able to dig and still find that you slip. You may find that affording the biggest house on the block is still out of your reach. Maybe the message is one of a more qijong nature: stop trying so hard. Conquering the world is hubris. It's a mistake. Maybe G-d gives us the illusion that we can achieve, succeed, and build, when in fact we are capable of nothing significant – only smoke and mirrors.

Can I conquer the world or am I confined to the realism of my space?

Success according to Judaism is living comfortably with the knowledge that I am capable of colossal achievement but G-d can, at any moment, tell us that a given space is not for us to conquer.

A statement of power emerges from the pen of ancient Jewish scholars: "May you always be the captain of your ship."[122] In other words, as the American novelist Louisa May Alcott put it, "I am not afraid of storms, for I am learning how to sail my ship."[123]

We are called upon to be bold and innovative. We are asked to become partners in creation. G-d is not content with us standing outside the fire. We are all captains. We are harbingers of change and difference.

Sometimes life seems to push back and tell us that we're not capable of making a difference. To that narrative we have to be forceful enough to say, "No!" The saintly Chassidic master the Bobover Rebbe lost everything in the Holocaust – family, friends, followers, disciples, and students. The Rebbe arrived in America after the war with nothing but the clothes on his back. The average human, after witnessing such destruction, would give credence to the push-back and live out his days in depression or apathy. The Bobover Rebbe was not willing to accept this fate. Piece by piece, brick by brick, he rebuilt first himself, then his family, and then an entire dynasty.

122 Leviticus Rabbah 21:5.
123 Louisa May Alcott, *Little Women* (Oxford: Oxford University Press, 1994), 82.

But then, when we are at our most powerful, when there is nothing that can get in our way – when we make decisions that seem to alter the course of destiny – G-d says, "Hold."

Here is where the line in the sand is drawn. Here is where you must set up your station. Moses had grand dreams of entering the land. He was an unlikely conqueror, a leader of men. He was humble, he was valiant, he kept leading and charting a new course when the tide was against him – but Israel, as the poet says, "that ever elusive dream," was no longer in the cards for Moses.

There is plenty of area for us all to master. There is no shortage of impactful space. But at some point G-d lets us know that our domain, our world, ends right at this point. The sages teach, "Who is happy? He who is content with his portion."[124] Happiness comes from harnessing the powers available to us within our orbit. What lies beyond our own personal domain is meaningless to our decisions. It's not our portion of the world. This thought may at first seem inhibiting but on the contrary, it's liberating. There is no room for jealousy when you don't have job X or house Y, because those positions and acquisitions are not even in your realm of existence.

Chart your course. Be bold, be strong, be creative, but know that at some point G-d can turn to you and say the words in our tradition that signal when a text is complete: "ad kaan" (until there).

Here is one bit of advice that may take us in a different direction. Sometimes a problem or a challenge is just that – a problem or a challenge. Often, a difficult situation allows us to rise above and bring out the best that we have hidden within. Other times, challenges evolve and ultimately become that wall where G-d says "until there." Perhaps we are capable of extending our reach if we make decisions before they become problems. Daniel Burrus, in his book *Flash Foresight*, argues that so many of our battles would cease to exist if we could learn to see the problem before it happens. If we can plan for success and see our hurdle before it arrives, we can better manage it. Turning a problem into

---

124 Ethics of the Fathers 4:1.

an opportunity is almost overwhelming once the problem has hit, and often it's too late. Become preactive. Preactive change (that is, action before a problem forces you to change) is a very powerful tool to help ensure, as best as possible, that you still have room to maneuver.[125]

The question you may ask, though, is how does one know whether the proverbial wall blocking you as you charge is synthetic and can still be traversed, or whether it is a wall that G-d has placed there to tell you, "until there"?

I would simply say that if the only way to scale that wall is by hurting others or by going against your moral compass, then you know it's the end of your space.

Kansas City Royals veteran Pitcher Gil Meche knew where his space ended. At thirty-two he walked away from a guaranteed $12.4 million. Why? He felt that after a series of injuries, he wouldn't be able to properly do the job. Taking that money would simply be wrong.[126]

Another way to know if you have come to the limit of your particular orbit is if the job at hand is asking you to compromise your identity, values, and/or your loved ones. No real long-term success can come about by trying to be somebody that you are not. Adjusting is always necessary to find true success, but to adjust to the extent that you no longer recognize yourself, or to the point where those who care most about you no longer recognize who you are, is a shift that G-d does not ask of you.

How do you know when it's your time to quit a particular job or a particular project? It is not an indicator when your job or investment hits a low point. The low point may in fact just be the great battle cry you need to make some shift that places you into the category of winners. Knowing when to quit is about recognizing what truly makes something a "low point." Am I no longer reaping value from what I set out to do? If

125 Daniel Burrus with John David Mann, *Flash Foresight: How to See the Invisible and Do the Impossible; Seven Radical Principles That Will Transform Your Business.* (New York: Harper Business, 2011).

126 Tyler Kepner, "Pitcher Spurns $12 Million, to Keep Self-Respect," *New York Times,* January 26, 2011.

my low point comes because I'm doing the same things I've always done and it's not working, that's not a sign to quit – that's a sign to try your job a little differently. But if your low point comes because you're not feeling the same invigoration you've always felt, then it may be a sign.

Another indication that it's time to stop pursuing the path you're on is when your current venture is capitalizing on all your weaknesses and ignoring most of your strengths. According to numerous sources, the ancient Egyptians who enslaved the Israelites employed an insidious trick to weaken the spirit of the people. They would give the men the jobs normally given to the women, and they would give the women jobs normally given to the men. When you're doing things that go against your nature, or just the things you are weakest at, it can literally tear you apart.

You also have to be careful about irrational behavior. Ori and Ron Brafman, in their book *Sway: The Irresistible Pull of Irrational Behavior*, make this case pretty clearly. At the beginning of their work they talk about an airplane pilot who took off in fog without getting clearance from traffic control. His plane crashed and over five hundred people (including the pilot himself) were killed. The tragedy is explained by irrational behavior. He considered all the negative consequences of leaving late or having to stay overnight, and all those trivial consequences meant more to him than departing safely.[127] We tend to fear the smaller, more immediate loss even at the possible expense of disaster. If a situation is simply not working but the only reason you're staying in it is because you're afraid of a new job hunt, or maybe being behind in your bills for several months, it's simply not worth your diminished quality of life, possible depression, and later regret for not having seized other opportunities. Know when you've hit the edge of your universe and respond accordingly.

127 Ori Brafman and Rom Brafman, *Sway: The Irresistible Pull of Irrational Behavior* (New York: Doubleday, 2008).

APPLYING "HOW TO KNOW WHEN TO WALK AWAY"

I will *know when to walk away* by making a commitment to take the following steps:

▸ I will acknowledge that I am capable of colossal achievement but G-d can, at any moment, tell me, "That space is not for you to conquer."

▸ I will chart my course. I will be bold, strong, and creative, but know that at some point G-d can turn to me and say, "*Ad kaan.*"

▸ By planning for success I will realize that I can see my hurdle before it arrives, which will allow me to better manage it.

▸ I will stop pursuing the path I'm on when my current venture is capitalizing on all my weaknesses and ignoring most of my strengths.

THE EVOLUTION – HOW TO MAKE PROGRESS EVERY DAY

You are either moving up up, or you are moving down down.
– The Gaon of Vilna

Behold the turtle. He only makes progress when he sticks his
neck out. – James Bryant Conant, *Harvard to Hiroshima and the
Making of the Nuclear Age*

It's no secret that the Torah has its issues with evolution, but is it
completely disturbed by an evolutionary concept? The founder of the
Chassidic movement, the Baal Shem Tov, makes a cryptic comment. He
says that the primary loss of the Jewish exile in Egypt was that *daas*
(knowledge) was in exile.[128] Without knowledge, which contributes to
our ability as human beings to speak, it follows that speech was also in
exile.

What does this mean, that *daas* was in exile? At the top of the
kabbalistic chain are three attributes: *chochmah* (wisdom), *binah*

---

128 *Sefer Baal Shem Tov*, vol. 2 (Jerusalem: Nofet Tzufim, 1987), 1.

(understanding), and *daas* (knowledge). These attributes are the big three and are known as "the mothers." *Chochmah* is the initial flash of energy when an idea first reaches the mind. *Binah* is when one begins to try to understand this flash of inspiration. *Daas* is when one tries to relate to this newfound information. Knowledge, then, is the ability to successfully integrate the material that we learn. This was temporarily lost while in Egypt.

The Torah teaches us: "*V'kol peter chamor tifdeh b'seh*" (there is an obligation to redeem each of your firstborn donkeys for a sheep).[129] Subsequent to this imperative, we are told, "*V'hayah ki yishalcha bincha machar leimor ma zos, v'amarta elav b'chozek yad hotzianu Hashem miMitzrayim, mi'beis avadim* (and when your son shall ask you, "What's this?" you will say to him that G-d took us out of Egypt with a strong hand from the house of slaves).[130] What's the connection between this verse and the aforementioned verse pertaining to the redemption of a donkey? Moreover, why did G-d command the Israelites that the firstborn donkey be exchanged for a sheep?

One great early twentieth-century scholar, Rav Yosef Dov Fishof, suggests that the answer lies in the distinction between a donkey and a sheep.[131] There is no animal used throughout history in greater proportion as a beast of burden than the donkey. The donkey works tremendously hard, doing the majority of load bearing. The food it is given is of the lowest quality, often poor quality scrub. The sheep, on the other hand, is treated as one the best among domesticated animals, for it has a faithful shepherd leading it through the greenest of pastures. When the Jewish people were in Egypt, they were at the level of donkeys, working literally like animals, day and night without stop. But G-d had different plans, and He eventually took them out and lifted them to the level of sheep. They also had a faithful shepherd in Moses, who led them in the right way. This is the connection between the two verses. The Egypt experience taught us that we must evolve.

129 Exodus 13:13.
130 Exodus 13:14.
131 Family tradition.

Momentum is the key to this development: taking one success and building toward another. In the business paradigm book *The Momentum Effect*, J. C. Larreche argues that for businesses to take the road to momentum, two factors must be in place: traction and movement.[132] Traction means that a product is in place that is so compelling that our movement in its direction is obvious and desired. Movement means that all possible obstacles in the way of ascertaining that prize product have been removed. For the Israelites, the slavery was removed. The backbreaking labor that distracted their resolve to live better was eliminated. Movement is enabled. Freedom in the form of the great Torah soon to be given at Sinai is the traction. Everything necessary for our development was now in place. A compelling product (Torah), a hungry people (the Israelites), and a path cleared of all obstacles.

The *Sefer Hachinuch* notes that on Pesach, the *korban ha'omer* (barley offering) is brought.[133] This is followed seven weeks later by the *shtei halechem* (two breads). Why? This is to symbolize our progression, going from animal food to human food, thus indicating that the Omer process is a time when we work on becoming humans. This is Jewish evolution. It is about bringing knowledge out of Exile (to use the words of the Baal Shem Tov). In Egypt we were made to feel almost subhuman. We lost the quality that distinguished us from animals – our ability to think freely.

Another component to this evolution is that one success breeds another. According to the Mishna, "*mitzvah goreres mitzvah*" (one good deed brings on another).[134] The classic Jewish philosophical work *Nefesh Hachaim* develops this idea with a metaphysical worldview. Each new good deed brings about a light, which is pure positive energy.[135] The pure positive energy attracts its kind and thusly brings about another mitzvah. One victory beckons the next. Outside of Kabbalah, is the "hot hand" for real? Can somebody on a winning streak expect a higher statistical

132 J. C. Larreche, *The Momentum Effect* (New Jersey: Prentice Hall, 2008).

133 Pinchas ben Yosef Halevi or Aaron ben Yosef Halevi, *Sefer HaChinuch* 310.

134 Ethics of the Fathers 4:2.

135 Chaim Ickovitz, *Nefesh Hachaim* 3:6.

probability of achievement on the next try? In a recent analysis at Yale University, researchers looked at an entire season of free throws. During a hot streak, researchers *did* find a significant jump in free throws made, above what was expected mathematically.[136]

There is a famous debate as to when the Israelites were commanded to build the Mishkan (Tabernacle). According to Rashi (Exodus 31:18), the commandment came after the sin of the golden calf. The Ramban assumes that the commandment to build the Tabernacle came before the sin of the golden calf.[137] The Ramban further develops the idea (35:1) that perhaps the commandment to build came before the tablets were broken. Once the second set of tablets were given, Moses commanded them once again.

What is the purpose of recapitulating a commandment after the second tablets? Moreover, why is the building of the Mishkan supposed to arise in context with the Sinai experience? Some suggest that the Mishkan was designed to be our personal Sinai wherever we may go. There's only one problem with this approach: Why not ask the Jewish people to build something that looks like Sinai, a mini mountain model, if you will? It is clear from numerous verses that the Mishkan was in fact supposed to look like a human being.[138] The Torah describes it in terms that are remarkably similar to human body parts. The reason for this is that the Tabernacle was supposed to reflect Sinai not in its appearance or structure, but rather in the sense that at Sinai we were learning how to become full-fledged human beings. Full-fledged meaning that we knew how to operate with *daas*, knowledge. As the Talmud in *Sotah* states, "there is no knowledge like the knowledge of Torah."[139] Therefore, the Israelites were implored to build an edifice that looked like a human being! Jewish evolution.

---

136 Gur Yaari and Shmuel Eisenmann, "The Hot (Invisible?) Hand: Can Time Sequence Patterns of Success/Failure in Sports Be Modeled as Repeated Random Independent Trials?" *PLoS ONE* 6, no. 10 (October 2011):1.

137 Nachmanides, *Peirush al Hatorah*, Exodus 25:1.

138 See Exodus 25:2, 5, 10, 20, 26, 31; 26:4, 14, 19, 20, 24.

139 Babylonian Talmud, *Sotah* 49a.

APPLYING "HOW TO MAKE PROGRESS EVERY DAY"

I will *make progress every day* by making a commitment to take the following steps:

▶ I will build momentum by stacking one good deed on top of another. I will harness the payoff of my victories to galvanize even better successes.

▶ I will acknowledge that I, as a human being, am in a constant state of evolution. I will recognize that my more base behaviors must be elevated, befitting a true *mentsch*.

The Path to the Side – How to Achieve Your Goals by Changing Your Approach

There's always another way. – The Kotzker Rebbe

If you do things well, do them better. Be daring, be first, be different, be just. – Anita Roddick

"There must be another way!" exclaimed Dai Vernon, the mysterious Canadian magician, as he was locked to a fence at a young age. Bullies had chained him there as a prank. "There must be another way." He went deep into his mind's eye and conjured up a unique maneuver to release himself from the fence. Freedom.[140]

There is almost always another way. It was the last few weeks of high school, and my mother told me that a great and saintly rabbi was staying at our neighbor's house. The Kaliver Rebbe, known for his piercing insight and his spiritual vision, was in town. I walked over. It was Friday afternoon. I waited for him in the backyard. He came out to meet me. There he was, resplendent and majestic in his special Sabbath garb, gold

---

140 David Ben, *Dai Vernon: A Biography; Artist, Magician, Muse*, vol. 1, 1894–1941 (Chicago: Squash, 2006).

and white. There was a still calmness on his worn face. I shook his hand
and he looked deep into my eyes. We stood there frozen for what felt like
minutes. And then he shared the following teaching with me.

As Moses approaches the burning bush, G-d tells him, "*Shal naa'lecha
me'al raglecha, ki hamakom asher atah omed alav admas kodesh hu*"
(Remove the shoes from your feet because where you stand is holy
ground).[141] This translation is the classic and accepted understanding
of the verse. However, explained the Kaliver Rebbe, there is a truth here
that is so much deeper, so much richer. The word for shoes in this verse
is *naa'lecha*. The same root forms the Hebrew word for "lock." It is even
used in modern Hebrew (*manul*). With this rendering the meaning
shifts: *Remove the locks/shackles from your feet, for if you realize that
no matter where you stand is holy ground, you are free.* Pow! I soared
through the sky like a comet when I heard that. You are never trapped;
there is always another way.

A couple struggling in a relationship often think that the only way to
freedom and happiness is by leaving each other, and sometimes that is
the case – but more often than not, there is another way. You may not
know it quite yet, and you may not notice the moment of insight, but
there can be another way for so many things that we do in life.

Steve Weinberg was driving to his office at MIT in the fall of 1976 when
something new about the forces of nature hit him. He was entering the
stage that is usually considered the end of one's prime for a theoretical
physicist. For years he had been trying to develop a theory of the strong
nuclear force (one of the four basic forces of nature), building upon the
theory of quantum electrodynamics (QED). But his effort to construct
a unifying theory simply wasn't working. On that drive, it dawned on
him – there must be another way. Instead of strong nuclear force, maybe
it was weak force, the force that causes neurons to shift into protons.
Weak force is critical for energy production in the world. It is at the root
of our survival. This flash of insight allowed Weinberg to develop what
was until then untouchable: a law of symmetry. Instead of giving up on
years of research, Weinberg knew – there was definitely another way.

141 Exodus 3:5.

It is said that some people like to hear stories so that they can go to sleep, while the seekers like to hear stories so they can wake up. Rebbe Nachman of Breslov had stories that – if you listened closely – would wake you up in a way that you'd never felt before. One of his great stories is "The Lost Princess,"[142] in which the title character goes missing after a quarrel with her father, the king. This tale of course is a metaphor. What does the lost princess symbolize? Lost innocence? Lost spirituality? Lost hope? There is no one answer. It is for the reader to find what speaks to him or her in the story. That's how Rebbe Nachman told stories.

At one point in the story, the valiant viceroy, who is sent on a long and difficult journey to find the princess, feels as though he is almost out of options. He is about to give up when he notices a path to the side. He collects himself and thinks, *Since I have been traveling for such a long time in the desert and I cannot find the princess, I will try this path – maybe it will bring me to a civilized area.*

Where is our path to the side? Strapped with financial burdens and medical challenges, often we find ourselves wondering how we dig ourselves out of such messes. Often, we try the same failed solutions over and over. We keep borrowing or gambling and push ourselves into deeper waters. We keep repeating the same mistakes in our parenting, thinking that this time around it's going to make a difference. But all along, there, off to the right, perhaps hidden by some trees, is your unique path to the side.

I remember meeting the friendliest human being you could ever meet. He lived each day with a smile. I would always bump into him in the street carrying his kids on his back. But behind that painted smile was the pain and pressure of making ends meet. This fellow, let's call him Simon, had a creative business idea that just fell apart. Then one bad deal after another. He would work late shifts at restaurants to make ends *not* meet. With only some change in his pocket, he was like a man possessed. Instead of the usual beeline he would make on his way home from work, he decided to stop into a local mini mart. He bought a lottery

142 Rebbe Nachman of Breslov, *Sippurei Maasiyot* (Jerusalem: Arvei Nachal Publishing, 1993), 34–42.

ticket and nailed it, and $6.3 million dollars later, he never forgets to be thankful for his path to the side.

A story like that isn't going to play out this way for most of us. The Powerball is not going to be our ticket out of suffering, but it does illustrate that there is a path to the side. The path looks different for each of us. You might find ironic the path of Rabbi Benjamin Blech. In his book *Taking Stock: A Spiritual Guide to Rising Above Life's Financial Ups and Downs*, Rabbi Blech mentions how his losing a million was actually his personal path to the side![143] I know what you're thinking – that's one side you'd like to avoid. Me too. But again, there is almost always an alternative way of doing things.

Eight hours after leaving Dai Vernon chained to that fence, the thugs came to the spot where they had tied him up. They found a pair of handcuffs, an empty soda can cut in half, and a bandana. But no Vernon. Where was he? How was this possible? They didn't know and neither do I. What is clear is that Dai Vernon had found his path to the side.

APPLYING "HOW TO CHANGE YOUR GOALS BY CHANGING YOUR APPROACH"

I will embody ultimate flexibility by making a commitment to take the following steps:

▶ I will review, research, and access the countless stories of people and organizations that have successfully reinvented themselves.

▶ I will develop a trust in G-d's ability to strengthen me as I try alternative strategies to find happiness and growth in my life.

---

143 Benjamin Blech, *Taking Stock: A Spiritual Guide to Rising Above Life's Financial Ups and Downs* (New York: Amacom, 2003).

Shoot for the Stars and Hold On to the Earth – How to Dream Big and Stay Grounded

The ladder was on the ground and its head was in the heavens.
– Genesis 28:12

Ruth came up in the fifth and, in no mistaken motions, the
Babe notified the crowd that the nature of his retaliation
would be a wallop right out of the confines of the park. – John
Drebinger, *New York Times*, October 2, 1932

One of the most famous moments in baseball history came during game three of the 1932 World Series against the Chicago Cubs. It was the fifth inning when Babe Ruth came up to bat. The count was two balls and two strikes. The formidable Charlie Root was on the mound. The mighty Babe did something that no Major League Baseball player had done before. He pointed to the center field bleachers. The pitch came down the pike and Babe Ruth bashed one of the longest home runs ever hit out of Wrigley Field, right above the spot he had pointed to.[144]

144 Ed Sherman, "81st Anniversary of Called Shot: The Media's View on Babe Ruth's Famous Homer," *Sherman Report*, October 1, 2013, http://www.shermanreport.com/81st-anniversary-of-called-shot-my-book-on-babe-ruths-famous-homer-coming-out-in-2014/.

This moment became the paradigm of mortal man reaching for the stars.

Often in our lives we hear the mantra "reach for the stars." The implication is that when setting goals, one should reach for the highest possible prize. On the other hand, we're familiar with the idea that when you hunt for two rabbits, you miss them both. This implies that we should make our goals more realistic, more down to earth, rather than somewhere catapulted into the stars.

Reaching for the stars means that we believe our ability is unlimited, we can do anything we like, and we can become as great as we want. It is a very American view of life: nothing can stand in the way of a dream. As the composer Antonio Salieri cries in Peter Shaffer's *Amadeus,* "I wanted to blaze like a comet across the sky."[145]

On the other hand, we want to be practical, realistic. We know all too well that trying to do too much leaves each area of pursuit unfulfilled. What is the Torah's approach to this dilemma – do we play it safe or do we set our sights on the greatest trophy?

The Talmud in *Sukkah* (5a) mentions the dictum *"tafasta merubeh, lo tafasta"* (One who grabs too much grabs nothing). This passage would seem to suggest a more tempered outlook on life. However, Maimonides says, "Don't think what the non-intelligent of the world think, that G-d decreed our future from the beginning. It's not so; rather humans can be as righteous as Moses."[146] Moses is one of the greatest heroes of the Bible. He is seen as the quintessential leader. Setting the bar with Moses means that we should in fact, in some sense make our aims tremendous.

Talk about lofty goals – we can be like Moses! What then of "one who grabs too much grabs nothing"? In order to develop a proper mystical approach, let us analyze these two sources closely.

1. *Tafasta merubeh lo tafasta.* One who grabs too much grabs nothing. When the Talmud uses this phrase it is in the context of ascertaining

---

145 Peter Shaffer, *Peter Shaffer's Amadeus* (New York: Perennial, 2001).
146 Maimonides, *Mishnah Torah*, Hilchot Teshuvah (Laws of Repentance) 5:1.

the height of the Ark in the Mishkan. The Talmud questions whether a metric for discovering the height of the Ark should be arrived at through a comparison with a bigger item in the Temple or a smaller item. To that end, the Talmud teaches us that one who grabs too much grabs nothing.

It's not about the quality of the goal, but the quantity. The mystical sources are teaching us that we should strive for greatness, we should seek to climb the highest mountain tops – but our goal for right now should be one mountain, one achievement; it is searching for too many goals and not having too high a goal that is the problem. Your goal can be great, but one step at a time. You can chase the fastest rabbit in the world, but only one at a time.

2. Humans can be as righteous as Moses. "Don't think what the non-intelligent of the world think," says Maimonides, "that G-d decreed our future from the beginning. It's not so." Does Maimonides' assertion that we can be as righteous as Moses place a limitless cap on our goals? Does Judaism promote setting goals way beyond our level, even to the point of absurdity? No. There is a limit. The great twentieth-century rabbi Elchanan Wasserman explains this passage from Maimonides.[147] The meaning of this law is that just as Moses fulfilled his potential, so can we can be like him in this very same way. We can reach our personal potentials.

The first source – one who grabs too much grabs nothing – teaches us that our goals should be tackled one at a time. On the other hand, Maimonides, as interpreted by Rav Elchanan Wasserman, teaches us that our goals need to take into account our potential.

In life we're asked not to reach for the stars, but to reach for our *personal* stars.

This Jewish approach is echoed in both scholarly research and current popular trends. The great child psychologist Dr. Bob Brooks explains that "Resilience embraces the ability of a child to deal more effectively with stress and pressure; to cope with everyday challenges; to bounce

---

147 Elchanan Wasserman, *Kobetz Maamarim* (New York: HaMeor, 1992), 13–14.

back from disappointments, adversity, and trauma; to develop clear and realistic goals; to solve problems; to relate comfortably with others; and to treat oneself and others with respect."[148]

When educating our children, if we set their bar way above their potential, then we set them up for failure and frustration; conversely, if we set the bar too low, they're never given a chance to emerge from their shell and develop their true selves.

In up-to-date psychology this approach finds sanction as well. From Dr. Phil to Zig Ziglar and many others, they all recommend a variation of a similar schema to the following:

1. Be specific.

2. Use measurable goals.

3. Assign a timeline to the goal.

4. Choose a goal that you can control.

5. Plan a program to get there.

6. Define a goal in terms of steps.

7. Create accountability.

Diet plans, programs for spiritual renewal and growth, 12 Step initiatives – these all fail when the goal is unrealistic or too much at once. We have to go step by step.

Let us test our hypothesis. Upon hearing about the many fantastic miracles of the Exodus, we cannot help but be overwhelmed by the enormity of the wonders that G-d performed for the Jewish people. To actually live through those remarkable events must have been the experience of a lifetime, something that would really transform a nation. How then are we to understand what happened next? Just after the flight from Egypt and Hashem's awesome revelation at Mount Sinai,

---

148 Robert B. Brooks and Sam Goldstein, *Raising Resilient Children with Autism Spectrum Disorders: Strategies for Helping Them Maximize Their Strengths, Cope with Adversity and Develop a Social Mindset* (New York: McGraw Hill, 2012), 4, © McGraw Hill Educational Material. All rights reserved. Used by permission.

the Jewish people worshipped a golden calf. How could they have fallen so far and so fast? *One who grabs too much grabs nothing.*

The Jewish people in the desert could not truly appreciate G-d's revelation because of the intensity and frequency of their spiritual experiences. They were bombarded with miracles. From the ten plagues in Egypt to the splitting of the Red Sea to the giving of the Torah, they witnessed the most remarkable miracles in history, and all in an extremely short span of time. They didn't have a chance to reflect on the enormity of these miracles and incorporate their message within themselves; they remained virtually unaffected by them. Miracles became an everyday occurrence, nothing special. As soon as anything went wrong, they were primed for a descent.

Trace the story of the great Rabbi Akiva. What were Akiva's beginnings? According to the source *Avos d'Rebbe Nosson* (chapter 1), up to the age of forty, he had not yet studied a thing. One time, while standing by the mouth of a well in Lydda, he inquired, "Who hollowed out this stone?" and was told, "Akiva, haven't you read in Scripture that 'water wears away stone' (Job 14:19)? It was water from the well falling upon it constantly, day after day." At that, Rabbi Akiva asked himself: "Is my mind harder than this stone? I will go and study at least one section of Torah." He went directly to a schoolhouse, and he and his son began reading from a child's tablet. Rabbi Akiva took hold of one end of the tablet, and his son took hold of the other end. The teacher wrote down *alef* and *bet* for him, and he copied them; *alef* to *tav*, and he learned them; the Book of Leviticus, and he studied it. He went on studying until he had grasped the whole Torah.

This passage, so reminiscent of *Shawshank Redemption*'s Andy Dufresne whose elaborate and gradual prison wall picking, little by little each and every day, one mountain at a time, bought him the freedom he had longed for.[149]

As the legendary John Wooden put it, "Mix idealism with realism and add hard work. This will often bring much more than you could

---

149 *The Shawshank Redemption*, directed by Frank Darabont, Burbank, CA, Columbia Pictures, 1994.

ever hope for."[150] Allow your dreams to soar. But measure them, know your potential, and take the path to your dream step by step.

150 John Wooden and Steve Jamison, *Wooden: A Lifetime of Observations and Reflections on and off the Court* (Lincolnwood, IL: Contemporary Books, 1997), 95.

Appendix

Seasonal Wisdom to Inspire

The Middle Way Is Killing You – The Month of Elul

An aha moment, according to Webster's dictionary, is a moment of sudden realization, insight, or comprehension. As we begin Elul,[151] how do we identify our aha moment? How do we pinpoint the paradigm shift that allows us to tackle the issues that keep us up at night, such as raising children, connecting with G-d in a meaningful way, finding financial success, and other struggles?

Recently Professor Jack Wertheimer in *Mosaic* magazine raised the elephant in the room question – can Modern Orthodoxy[152] survive?[153] This spurred a response from writers at all ends of the spectrum. The question is disturbing to those of us who are interested in a serious Judaism that is fully committed to the Torah and its sages and who at the same time are not afraid to engage the modern world and totally

---

151 Elul is the final month on the Jewish calendar.

152 For the purpose of this essay I will define Modern Orthodox as the orientation of Jews who believe in the dictates of Torah, Talmud, and *halachah* and also believe they are compatible with an integrated modern worldview.

153 Jack Wertheimer, "Can Modern Orthodoxy Survive?" *Mosaic* magazine, August 3, 2014, http://mosaicmagazine.com/essay/2014/08/can-modern-orthodoxy-survive/.

encourage and support the State of Israel – we wonder, is there a future for this fascinating and small demographic?

Let us leave our questions behind for the moment and explore an idea that may give us *chizuk* during this great month. In 1976, Philip Glass and Robert Wilson premiered an opera called *Einstein on the Beach*. It lasted five hours, and audience members were invited to come in and walk out at will. Movements within the opera repeated over and over, dance numbers went on for extended periods of time. As Robert Wilson said of *Einstein on the Beach*, "It's a work where you can go and get lost. That's the idea."[154] The creative concept was to have the audience lose themselves entirely to the piece.

When I reflect upon the opera of *Einstein on the Beach* I think about what our Judaism wants of us. It doesn't want our partial and lukewarm engagement. G-d wants us to lose ourselves within the experience. We don't just coldly shake a *lulav* (the palm frond waved during the holiday of Sukkos). We are asked to live the mandate and meaning behind the *lulav*. In a sense, G-d wants us totally immersed. Even the simplest mitzvah and the most common act of living should be committed with intensity and passion.

The great mystic rabbi in Bnei Brak the Koidenover Rebbe interprets the Torah's words "*Shoftim v'shotrim titen lecha b'chol she'arecha*" (Judges and officers you shall place at all of your gates)"[155] as meaning, "Observance and commitment should be placed at all the 'gates,' all the vistas of our lives."[156] Judaism is not just reserved for our relatively few moments in shul. No, we must be totally invested. Judaism is alive when we sit down for breakfast, Judaism is being experienced when we help our children with their homework. It's always vibrating in every part of our life.

---

154   Jim Farber, "'Einstein on the Beach' in L.A. is a Historic and Harmonic Convergence," *Los Angeles Daily News*, October 7, 2013, http://www.dailynews.com/arts-and-entertainment/20131007/einstein-on-the-beach-in-la-is-a-historic-and-harmonic-convergence/1.

155   Deuteronomy 16:18.

156   Heard in the name of the Koidenover Rebbe.

To bring a less reverent metaphor, the radical nineteenth-century German philosopher Friedrich Nietzsche presented an illustration of a camel, a lion, and a child.[157] The camel unquestioningly bears the load of that which is placed upon it, the lion rips apart all that dare stand in its way, but the child learns how to live comfortably with the load of the past and the uncertain tempest that the future may bring. A meaningful and heart-pumping Judaism knows how to comfortably bring forward our past legacy, heritage, and identity and integrate it with a strange modern world. This world we exist in now is a foreign one for the wandering Jew, but when we are totally immersed in our Judaism and it is in every part of our lives, the unknown becomes a bit more knowable. Our past informs our future, and our future is an opportunity for bringing Judaism to a world that is thirsty for its influence.

Being a Jew in the modern world doesn't mean that we are committing ourselves to a middle way. The middle way is *pareve*, boring, and insipid. We are proud and we are strong because we carry the totality of time as we move through it. I recently picked up a new *sefer* that is over three hundred pages of halachic analysis on issues that have newly risen because of the Internet. Projects like this reflect the way that our tradition is meant to be totally and not partially lived. Judaism is not a 9 to 5 experience.

The laws of *dayanus* (judging) at the beginning of the important halachic compilation *Choshen Mishpat* indicate a clear imperative to choose *peshara* – loosely translated as "settlement." Rav Yehoshua Falk, known as the Sema, insists that a *peshara* is not about some middle-way agreement that undermines the true will of both parties.[158] No, it is a more complete way that honors and respects the narratives of both claimant and respondent. This is the Jewish way.

---

157 Friedrich Nietzsche, *Thus Spoke Zarathustra* (New York: Penguin Classics, 1962), 111–12.

158 Yehoshua Falk, *Commentary on Choshen Mishpat* 9:3.

The Rambam notoriously emphasized the *shevil hazahav*, the golden mean.[159] He never meant the boring middle. Rather, the Rambam referred to a balance that honors both ends of a given spectrum.

There is a wonderful book called *Shteigen* filled with anecdotes and sources aimed at building greater enthusiasm for learning Torah. Let me share with you a stark illustration used in the book.[160] Imagine a waiter at an amazing wedding. He hears the dynamic band, he gets to taste the same delicious food, and he sees the same important people that everybody else at the wedding gets to see. But something is different. He's estranged, detached, removed. Why? Because he isn't truly part of the celebration. He is there but he is not there.

This "waiter story" nails the necessity of our full engagement and integration with our Jewish experience. We can't stand on the sidelines watching our *mitzvos* go by. We can't just robotically go through the motions of Shacharis like impartial observers. We need to fully integrate the experience. Why are we davening? Who are we davening to? Go totally in.

Our effort to be in the middle is simply killing us. Our effort to be neutral, "modern," or "normal" is sucking the life out of our experience. Living as a Modern Orthodox Jew is not about being in the middle or in one space in the Jewish time continuum; it's about living with Hashem fully in *everything* that we do.

In the month of Elul, we observe the *yahrzeit* of the saintly Rav Avraham Yitzchak HaKohen Kook. Rav Kook in his *Orot HaKodesh* writes that the great *tzaddikim* are the ones who see the world in all of its beauty and respect it. They see the exaltedness of the world. They don't look around and say, "*Feh*, this world is unkosher." They look at history, at art, at creativity and notice the awesome power that Hashem has bestowed onto humanity. They notice that even among the backdrop of intense horror there is a tremendous capacity for love and healing.

---

159 Maimonides, *Mishnah Torah*, Hilchot De'ot (Laws of Personal Development) 1:5.

160 Elazar Moskowitz, *Shteigen* (Bnei Brak: Hatikra, 2012), 117–18.

The *tzaddik*'s Judaism is total and complete; it embraces the light of the entire world.

This is our aha moment. It's the realization that the best shot we have at our struggles and challenges is to live with a holistic Yiddishkeit. Hashem is our advisor in shul but also in school, on Wall Street, and on the street.

I'd like to close with a very moving story. Rabbi Aryeh Zev Ginzberg of the Chofetz Chaim Torah Center in Long Island related the following story.[161] The son of one of his congregants went to learn in Israel and decided to enroll in a *hesder yeshiva*. In the summer of 2005, during the Gaza Disengagement, the army had to forcibly remove Jewish settlers who refused to leave. This American soldier was very distraught about the assignment, but as a soldier he followed orders and participated in the forced evacuation.

When his unit arrived at one of the settlements, his job was to ensure that the settlers boarded the buses to be evacuated. He worked in tandem with the rabbi of the settlement. The settlers gathered in the town's synagogue where the rabbi spoke, followed by the soldier. They all wept together, before filing out of the synagogue and boarding the bus.

Before the bus left, this soldier took out a *siddur* (prayer book) from his backpack, dug a hole, and buried it there. When the rabbi asked him why he was doing so, he replied that perhaps at some point in the future someone would return and might find the *siddur*, and would realize that they had left begrudgingly, and that they left their hearts and prayers behind.

Eleven months later, in the summer of 2006, Gilad Schalit was captured by Hamas militants in Gaza. When Israel decided to reinvade Gaza in an attempt to find him, the unit of that American soldier was sent back into Gaza to set up a base of operations. They entered Gaza under the cover of darkness, and although they did not know exactly where they were, they set up camp in a deserted area. The next morning, the soldier looked around, disoriented, not recognizing anything. Everything had been destroyed. Still he knelt down on the ground and started digging. To his shock he found the *siddur* he had buried.

He was shaken by the experience and called his father in America to recount to him the uncanny story. He asked his father to ask his rabbi to interpret the significance of what had occurred.

Rabbi Ginsberg himself was mystified by the story and arranged for the soldier to have a private meeting with Rav Chaim Kanievsky. Rav Chaim asked him what he did when he found out that he would have to evict the settlers. The soldier replied that he had begged his commanding officers to abandon their plans, and he prayed fervently that the evacuation be aborted. Rav Chaim then asked him what he did when he found out that he would have to proceed with the evacuation. The soldier replied that once he was told they were going ahead with it, he stopped praying for it not to happen.

Rav Chaim replied that G-d was sending him a message that one should never stop praying! "You buried the *siddur* because you felt it was futile to continue to pray. G-d returned it to you so you should realize that it's never too late, or too hopeless, to pray."

There is much to take away from the story, but what I see in it is that Rav Chaim Kanievsky understood that prayer is not an on-and-off occupation. With prayer, we are all in. There is no middle way; there is only the complete way, in which every experience of our lives is worth a prayer.

Let us live our Elul fully and in that merit may there arrive a truly life-changing Rosh Hashanah.

SWEET TREATS FOR ROSH HASHANAH

Rosh Hashanah is a time of tremendous renewal and creativity.[162] The potential for innovation and great paradigm shifts is magnified as Elul progresses. We need this powerful capability for rejuvenation so that we can fulfill the primary function of the shofar according to the Rambam: "Even though the shofar blowing is mandated by the Torah, it is also hinted in the matter of 'Wake up, you sleepers, from your slumber.'"[163] Our personal attachment to Judaism needs to be alive and vibrant, and what better way to arouse our spirituality than to share new insights into the High Holidays?

LIFE IS A BATTLEFIELD

The Koidenover Rebbe, Rav Yaakov Tzvi Ehrlich, explains "*Ki seitzei la'milchamah*" (When you go out to battle…) metaphorically.[164] We are all creatures of habit. We wake up and go about our morning routines in the same way each and every day. Those patterns and recurring behaviors are helpful when the activities that we repeat are beneficial. For example, praying each day is wonderful and healing. But what if

---

162 See Rav Shmuel Auerbach, *Ohel Rachel* (Jerusalem: Ateres, 2004), Elul, 34.

163 Maimonides, *Mishnah Torah*, Hilchot Teshuvah (Laws of Repentance) 3:4.

164 Tzvi Ehrlich, *Nachalei Orah Journal* 34 (2012): 182.

the habits and behaviors that are so much part of our routine no longer seem to be helping us? What about the fact that our impulse to talk negatively about somebody else is so ingrained in our daily dialogue that we can't seem to shake it?

Says the Koidenover Rebbe, we need to live life at war. We need to live in a state of dissatisfaction with our situation. We need to be moved by the impulse to fight over and over again for what we know to be right. "Even thirty times a day." Even if we fall, we need to get up and prepare ourselves like soldiers so we can perform our *avodah*, our holy service. In this Yomim Noraim season the Koidenover Rebbe's words are emboldening. Gird yourself and fight the good fight because changing an unwanted behavior is war.

You Gotta Start Somewhere

The iconic Chassidic figure Rav Zushe of Anipoli, brother of Reb Elimelech, always understood that change is hard. He explained that once we make a true accounting of where we stand with our deeds and sins, we will shudder when thinking about the delta we need to cross as we travel from where we are to where we should be. The solving of a misdeed and the prospect of doing *teshuvah* may be too overwhelming.

In order to make it more manageable, we must start simply with the "beginning of *teshuvah*." What is the beginning of *teshuvah*? *Teshuvah* in Hebrew is spelled תשובה. Start with the beginning, ת-ש-ו. Those letters, *taf, shin, vav*, stand for the three phrases *tamim tihyeh im Hashem Elokecha* (you should be sincere with Hashem your G-d), *shivisi Hashem l'negdi samid* (I will place G-d in front of me constantly), and *ve'ahavta l're'acha k'mocha* (and you should love your neighbor as yourself).

Rav Zushe argues that the best place to start is with the core tenets of our relationship with G-d. Step one is sincerity in our relationship with Hashem. Be honest and be real. we mustn't turn our Judaism into *shtick*. Step two, placing G-d in front of us at all times, means that in all of my troubles and triumphs, G-d is a part of my conscious being. Rebbe Menachem Nachum of Chernobyl was known for his piety and profound prayers. One day his students overheard him praying, "G-d, please, the housekeeper who assists my wife, please put in her mind not to leave us." Upon hearing this, his students turned to him and asked, "This is what the great master prays for?" The Rebbe's answer is so simple and so utterly earthshaking: "And to whom else should I turn to if not G-d?"[165] Finally, step three is to love your neighbor: G-d wants our divine repair to start with mending our relationships below. We can't possibly be distant from our friends and family, yet be close to G-d. Judaism does not accept the vision of a prophet detached on a mountaintop. Only when we are "one people with one heart" do we deserve the Torah.

The Mitzvah to Delete a Mitzvah

Perhaps the cornerstone mitzvah of this time of the year is the mitzvah of *teshuvah*, repentance. The Ramban writes that the source for this mitzvah is Deuteronomy 30:11. The wording of the Rambam, however, seems to indicate that *teshuvah* is not an independent mitzvah.[166] The *Minchas Chinuch* feels that the Rambam assumes *teshuvah* to be part of the mitzvah of *vidui* (confession). Other Achronim suggest that the Rambam doesn't list *teshuvah* independently because it is a component of every mitzvah.

There is something fascinating about this mitzvah. If *teshuvah* is adhered to in its ideal sense, then effectively we could delete this mitzvah. Let me explain. If I perform the mitzvah of eating *matzah*, no matter how well I fulfill this mitzvah the opportunity will return the following year. That is true, albeit with variation, for every mitzvah. Nevertheless, when it comes to the mitzvah of *teshuvah*, the irony is that the better I am at completely repairing what I did wrong, the less *teshuvah* will need to be done. With enough work and with enough strength, hypothetically, we can actually remove a mitzvah from our list. Yes, it is true that nobody is perfect on this earth, but I find it fascinating that *teshuvah* is the singular mitzvah that is designed to be phased out.

---

165 Moshe Wolfson, *V'ani Tefilah* 4.
166 Maimonides, *Mishnah Torah*, Hilchot Teshuvah (Laws of Repentance) 1:1.

On one hand, there is no question here. It could simply be that G-d would create one mitzvah that He challenges us to perfect to such a level that there is no need for it. But it strikes me that this is not the case. Why would all 612 other *mitzvos* have one design while *teshuvah* stands as an outlier? We can suggest that there are two aspects to *teshuvah*: *azivas chet* (leaving the sin behind us) and *kirvas Elokim* (coming close to G-d). If *teshuvah* is translated as "repentance" or the making right of something we did wrong, then our question will still stand. But if *teshuvah* is true to its etymology, "return," then *teshuvah* is marked by our connecting with Hashem. And if the defining marker is coming close to our Maker then there is no end to this mitzvah.

BEHIND A CAGE

Many of the classic Elul *mussar schmuessen* make use of the homily presented by the *Shelah*. The *Shelah* cites the verse in Amos (3:8), "*Aryeh sha'ag; mi lo yira?*" (The lion roars; who will not fear?). He takes the word *aryeh* (lion) and breaks it down into *alef* for Elul, *resh* for Rosh Hashanah, *yud* for Yom Kippur, and *heh* for Hoshanah Rabbah, the four main phases of renewal during this time. The message is that with such an intense influence of holiness and opportunity, who can help but awaken with reverence and passion as one would upon hearing the call of the lion?

Rav Elyashiv takes this thought one step further. "The lion roars; who will not fear." That *pasuk* is meant to be read rhetorically. However, adds Rav Elyashiv, in our generation it can be read as a question with an answer. Who will not fear the lion's roar? A person who hears the lion roar at a zoo. There the majestic scream of the lion causes us to tremble a little less because the lion is locked behind bars. Rav Elyashiv says that in our modern world we have locked our hearts inside a cage of skepticism, coldness, and distance. When the lion roars we don't tremble as we should.

What a powerful call initiated by Rav Elyashiv. Unlock our hearts and set them free to be truly present for our religious experiences. Stale Judaism has no place on Rosh Hashanah. Awaken and arise!

AND A STORY

I'd like to close with a fantastic story buried in the great work *Derech Hamelech* by Rav Kalonymus Kalman Shapiro of Piaseczna.[167] I will leave the story open ended. Find your own meaning within.

Once upon a time, there was a king who ruled over many lands and peoples. Some of them were close to his castle and some were on lands that were far away. There was one group of people who lived on distant mountains. They were known to be wild and barbaric. These people ate weird and foul foods and dressed in strange rags with animal hides. They were known to be dangerous, but the king gathered his noblemen together and declared, "One of you must go to the wild people and rule them in my name." All the noblemen shook their heads and refused. They were too afraid to go.

Finally the king turned to the prince, his beloved son. "Maybe you will go and be the new ruler of the wild people?" he asked. "Yes, Father," answered the son, "I will go but with two conditions. You must help me whenever I need assistance, and if I really get into trouble, you must come in person." "By all means!" agreed the king. "Yes! I promise to help you."

So the king's son traveled to the distant land of the wild people. At first, it was very difficult for him. Their food was vulgar and not at all like the delicacies he ate in the king's palace. The clothing was strange and rough, not at all like the beautiful, soft clothing he had worn in his father's court. Despite this, as time passed he slowly grew used to the ways of the wild people. And, of course, he wrote letters to his father, reporting on his progress and telling him how much he missed him. As time went on, he slowly managed to take charge of this strange people and their distant lands. However, the prince then began to forget the language he had spoken in the palace. Soon, he could not remember the courtly language at all, and that is when the trouble began.

167 Kalonymus Kalman Shapiro, *Derech HaMelech*, trans. David Rovin (New York: HaMeor, 2001), 313.

Even though the prince was a good man, he had enemies. Whenever he wrote letters to the king in the language of the wild people, his enemies would open them before they were sent to the king. The enemies changed the contents and erased the sentences about the prince missing his father, the king. Once or twice, the prince succeeded in convincing his father to come and inspect the land of the wild people. "I hope he will come and we will spend some time together," said the prince.

The king made the long journey and hoped to see his son, but the enemies made sure that the son would be somewhere else on official business so he would miss the visit of his father, the king. The son became very sad. He had no idea what his enemies were doing to him, but he did know that he wanted to see his father and he was very upset that he could not remember the language of the palace and how the delicious food tasted or how the beautiful clothes felt. Most of all, he missed his father.

One day, he was sitting in his office all alone and feeling very sad, when he remembered that his father had given him something very special. "When you are in trouble," said the king to his son, the prince, before he left, "and you need me to come in a hurry, just take out this magical bell. Ring the bell loudly and I will come." The prince jumped out of his chair and ran to the cupboard and started to search for the magical bell. He grabbed fists full of papers and threw them over his shoulders as he dug deeper and deeper into all of the things stored in the cupboard. Finally, he found the bag with the magic bell. He took it out and with a big smile on his face and a tear in his eye, he rang the bell. The prince was happy that he had finally rung the bell, but he was still sad that the king was so far away. Feeling hopeless, he sat down and buried his head in his hands.

Suddenly, he felt a hand on his shoulder and when he looked up, he saw the king. The magic had worked and his father had come to visit him. The king sat down at the table next to his son and the prince began to explain why he had rung the bell. "I was not in any real danger, but I missed you so much. I was hoping that you would come often to visit me. I even invited you many times but you did not come." Then the prince began to cry.

The king explained to his son how the wild people had changed his letters and even when he did come, the wild people kept the prince away from him. This brought his son to tears again. "Father, I really don't care that I have to eat their terrible food or dress in their strange clothes. I am here to work for you, my father, my king. But I am so unhappy because you are so far away from me." The king gave his son a hug and promised to visit his son more often. And so the king returned to his palace and his son, the prince, went happily back to work.

THINGS DO FALL APART

When the cold winter creeps in, the warm embrace of the Yomim Noraim, the High Holidays, starts to fall by the wayside. All our prayers, the learning, each busy moment that we filled with *avodas Hashem*, can too quickly evaporate and we are left with the cold chill of a weekday morning.

Try to leave your *sukkah* alone and you'll notice within a short amount of time, as African writer Chinua Achebe puts it, "things fall apart." Not only does the *cheftza*, the physical sukkah, break down, but within a very short time the *gavra*, our individual spiritual dimension, can fall apart as well. Yet, it is that way by design. The opinion holds true, *sukkah diras ara'i b'inan* – a *sukkah* should be temporary.[168]

The Rebbe of Stichin questions our ability to properly ascertain our spiritual fall. Though we may return to our old ways after Sukkos, we likely have no clue as to how profound was the spiritual change within. If we could grasp this positive insight, it would help us through the insurmountable challenge and impending failure that we sense with our exit from the *sukkah* and the onset of winter.

In my humble opinion, the new cycle of the *parshah*, which ironically coincides with the end of the holidays, beckons us to find solace and

---

168 Babylonian Talmud, *Sukkah* 7b.

wisdom from the start of this post–*yom tov* world that envelops us. The Book of Genesis is really the genesis of our experience. The first five *parshiyos* form a road map for this journey.

BEREISHIS: HOW WE RELATE TO OUR MISTAKES DECIDES OUR NEXT CHAPTER

The Torah begins with G-d's creation of the world and humanity's subsequent failure to live up to our own expectations. This first powerhouse *parshah* is not so much about messing up, it's more about how we choose to handle our foibles. Eve touches the tree and decides to degrade further. Adam blames his wife. The snake refuses repentance. Cain attempts to hide from G-d. We are created as imperfect human beings. G-d knows that we are going to make mistakes. The distinction between the strong and the weak is in how we get up from our fall.

There's a remarkable fact about Koheles, or Ecclesiastes, one of the books written by King Solomon that is in our cannon. The rabbis, according to the Talmud, came very close to banning it from our tradition. In the end, it prevailed because "it starts and ends with Torah." What does that mean?

Because something starts okay and ends okay, it's worth keeping as a masterpiece of our tradition. But our sages are telling us something far more profound. The apparent flaws of Koheles are representations of our own shortcomings. We are at times heretical, we are at times contradictory. Nevertheless, we know how to pick ourselves up and straighten our path. We are Koheles. We are worth keeping.

Perhaps this is also the explanation of why we begin Yom Kippur with the nighttime prayer that has us asking for permission "to pray with the sinners." Which sinners are we asking to pray with? Are we so perfect that we need to check in with G-d before davening with other people? The "sinner" we refer to is actually the flawed part of ourselves. Accepting our shortcomings and growing from them is an essential component of the *kapparah*, the atonement process.

What we choose to do with our past will always dictate our future. Our personal legacy shifts because of the empowering choices we make.

Should we interpret our past history of being overly critical of others as a behavior set in stone? Or do we make a choice to stop patterns of speech that push people away?

NOACH: DESTRUCTION BEFORE RENEWAL

Noach is the story of one man's ability to hold on to morality in the face of tremendous evil. When G-d brings about the deluge, Noach indulges the darkness and finishes his life by interpreting disaster as the end. But it's not the end. Destruction must come before renewal. After darkness there must be sun. The Jewish understanding of *yom*, the day, follows this format: night and then light.

When we sleep, we experience a taste of death (*Berachos* 57a), and therefore by extension a microcosm of decomposition. This reboot is necessary for us to reignite a passion for another day. As the code of Jewish law the *Shulchan Aruch* opens by charging, "*Yisgaber k'ari la'amod ba'boker la'avodas Boro*" (Let one wake up like a lion in the morning to serve one's Creator). Rebbe Nachman says, that each morning when we wake there is a part of us that is the lion, there is a part of us that has done something strong the day before.[169] Find that point and use that to begin the new day with vigor.

There may be nothing more unsettling in life than the loss of a position at a company or the implosion of a project that we have worked on for years. But we must know that this kind of obstruction is more than just a setback, it is the opportunity for a new set of *luchos* (tablets) to emerge into the world, a set that is formed by the blood, sweat, and tears available because of our partnership with G-d.

In *Thus Spoke Zarathustra*, Nietzsche tells us, "The snake that cannot shed its skin perishes. So do the spirits who are prevented from changing their opinions; they cease to be spirit." Profound and true. We tumble before we rise.

---

169 *Likutei Halachos* 1, 55.

Lech Lecha: Jump into Our Challenges, Don't Run from Them

Lech Lecha is the accounting of Abraham's life in the wake of his "come to G-d" moment at home. His family, his community, and his social circle were all immersed in idolatry. Abraham has an intense epiphany (a *bira dolekes* – a burning palace, as the Midrash has it), and this is where he recognizes ethical monotheism. Armed with this knowledge, he finds his outlook on life now conflicts with everybody on his side of the universe. Abraham is faced with an enormous challenge: Should he hold back the urge to change the world or should he find the courage to fight the tide?

Abraham is not Yonah. Yonah ran from his mission to rebuke the people. Abraham made friends with his demons. He acknowledged his past that was steeped in idolatry, and this is what drove his future. He knew that our world was uncertain and he could feel there was some great power out there. He was grateful to face his fears. His challenge was to bring his monotheistic epiphany to a world that was steeped in paganism and the occult. He didn't run from this noble calling. *Lech lecha* – he ran to this task with audacity.

This is how Rav Soloveitchik interprets the passage in *Yoma* 86b, that with *teshuvah* our trespasses turn to merits. Is this magic or are we able to take our challenges, our struggles, and our past darkness as a point of departure for all our new experiences? The same energy we used to violate our covenant with G-d should now be used to reignite our relationship with G-d.

Think how easy it is to push off pending work. We prefer to task ourselves with picking the low-hanging fruit rather than slaving to achieve mastery of all our fields. Lean in to your challenge. Social psychologist Gary Keller says we need to find that one achievement each day that lets us achieve our greatest potential. Leave the lesser things for another time.

Vayeira: Be Grateful for Our Fear

Vayeira's legacy will always be the binding of Isaac. This penultimate test is the greatest of all. For Abraham, this test manipulated his biggest fear.

Abraham had long worried about leaving a legacy, having somebody to whom he could entrust the gift of ethical monotheism. When G-d called upon him to offer his son, he knew the mission would annihilate his dream. Yet Abraham passes the test and immediately offers an animal to Hashem. Why? Abraham has the wisdom to show gratitude to G-d for his fear. Abraham understands that our greatest fears are opportunities for life-changing experiences for growth and development.

Jonathan Haidt in his book *The Happiness Hypothesis* stresses that "adversity may be necessary for growth because it forces you to stop speeding along the road of life, allowing you to notice the paths that were branching off all along, and to think about where you really want to go."[170] Be grateful for your speed bumps.

Chayei Sarah: Why We Daven

The last piece for now is to think about *why* we spent so much time davening over Rosh Hashanah/Yom Kippur/Sukkos. The purpose of this intense holiday period was never intended to be permanent detachment from the world. Quite the opposite. The purpose is to develop and cultivate our inner space so that we are better equipped to face the turbulence of life and the clutter of our minds. Eknath Easwaran in his book on meditation, *Conquest of Mind,* tells us that "Meditation is warm-up exercise for the mind, so that you can jog through the rest of the day without getting agitated or spraining your patience."[171] *Tefillah,* prayer, is *charbi u'vkashti* (Genesis 48:22) – our sword and arrow for life.

We should understand that our motivation for improvement and change is not only for ourselves but also so we can be in a better emotional state when dealing with others. Our efforts in shul are for our spouses, our children, and our bosses. The moment we step out of shul is the moment we are finally allowed to put everything into practice.

---

170 New York: Basic Books, 2006, 166.

171 *Conquest of Mind: Take Charge of Your Thoughts and Reshape Your Life through Meditation* (Tomales, CA: Nilgiri Press, 2010), 32.

In Chayei Sarah, Abraham purchases Me'aras Hamachpeilah. According to the *Zohar*, Abraham looked into the cave and saw the window for prayer in this world. He saw a place of such intense energy. He saw the gateway to Shabbos. I once heard the Kaliver Rebbe of Bnei Brak ask why Efron sold the land for so little if there was such divine light emanating from the cave. He answered that it took somebody as special as Abraham to perceive this *kedushah*. Once Abraham recognized the light in Me'aras Hamachpeilah, he could have rested there for the remainder of his life. Did he? He could not because that *hashpaah*, that influence was a gift. It was time to take that gift and come back to the world. There was still so much work left for him to do.

CONCLUSION

When the oasis of sanctity called Tishrei retreats, our imperfect selves become apparent once again. But that's okay; things fall apart. We learned from the Yomim Noraim in a more striking way how to relate to our mess, how to appreciate that destruction comes before rebirth, how to jump into our mess, how to be grateful for our fear, and to understand why we spent so much time davening.

TOWARD AN UNDERSTANDING OF MYSTICAL TIME – CHANUKAH

Rebbe Nachman often speaks about the power of *dimyon* (imagination). In that spirit he stokes our imagination with a powerful Chanukah image. Rebbe Nachman says that life is like a spinning dreidel. Sometimes we keep landing on *shin* and seem to never catch a break. Other times our lives are partially fulfilling and in that sense we have landed on *heh*. This evocative illustration leads us to develop three conceptions of our engagement with or perception of time: How do the days of our lives play out?

LIFE IS LIKE A DREIDEL

One engagement that we have with time is in the way just expressed by Rebbe Nachman. Life is like a dreidel. Life is a seemingly random spin of the wheel. Ray Billington, in his discussion of moral philosophy, compares this outlook with the image of a bag filled with nails.[172] Shake up the bag and the result is random and chaotic. This is one perception of time. The shortsightedness of this perception is that it ignores that great Hand controlling the dreidel. The Dinover Rebbe distinguishes

172 *Religion without God* (London and New York: Routledge, 2001), 101.

between the control of a Purim *gragger* where the handle is below and the Chanukah *dreidel* where the handle is above. G-d's Hand in the Chanukah story is open and revealed.

THE MAHARAL'S SPIRAL

We may be familiar with another type of engagement with time. When the angels come to Abraham in his tent to bring him news, we are told that he was making cakes. The Midrash clarifies that he was in fact preparing matzos. Why? Because it was Pesach. How is that possible? The Exodus from Egypt and entry to Israel hadn't even happened yet! The Maharal explains that our difficulty is predicated upon a faulty assumption. We assume that time moves linearly. Event A (the Exodus) transpires and this leads us to commemorate it with certain rituals year after year. This is incorrect. Event A happens because embedded in creation is the reality that this specific day is imbued with a power for renewal and redemption. The Exodus was able to happen because of the potential inherent in this time. Not the opposite. And time does not move forward repeating the same point each year; rather we repeat the same point but we visit it from a different plane.

This is the significance behind the Rambam's almost direct quote of the Gemara: "One is obligated to see himself as though he is leaving *right now* from Egypt." The Seder evening is not an exercise in memory or pretending. Rather it's an opportunity to revisit that same point in time but on a different level of the spiral.

THE VILNA GAON'S UPWARD MOVEMENT

The Vilna Gaon writes that if we are not moving up, then by necessity we are moving down. There is no staying in one place.

After numerous years of studying the most sublime Torah in the Yeshiva of Shem and Ever, Jacob takes his first sleep in a long time. When he rests on the rock, we read about how he saw angels climbing down and up a ladder. Angels make another appearance in Jacob's life when he is leaving the house of Lavan. We are not told about the function of this second set of angels. What is the Torah trying to teach us? The late

Har Etzion *rosh yeshiva* Rav Aharon Lichtenstein says that the Torah is underscoring the passion and drive of Jacob. The fact that he dreamed of angels after studying Torah day and night is no surprise. But what does Jacob dream of after living with a swindler like Lavan? Is he still dreaming of greatness and angel? Does he still have a longing for glory? The answer is unequivocally yes.

"Who is wise? He who learns from everyone." So says the Tanna in Ethics of the Fathers (4:1). What did Jacob learn from Lavan after spending many years there? Rashi gives us a window into his experience at Lavan's house. Jacob's opening words to his brother Esau in their encounter are "*Im Lavan garti*" (I was living with Lavan). Rashi adds: "I was living with Lavan and I kept the 613 commandments and I didn't learn from Lavan's wicked ways." At face value it sounds like Jacob didn't learn a thing from Lavan. However, there is another way to read this Rashi. Rav Yehoshua Berkowitz, former rabbi of Shaarei Tefilah, suggests the following read: "I didn't learn from Lavan's wicked ways" *but* "I did learn from his good ways." Perhaps Lavan's passion for wickedness and deceit was something to be adopted into Jacob's practice of mitzvos. Perhaps Jacob learned to live with passion. This interpretation would explain why he was interested in delivering this message to Esau. Jacob was letting his brother know that was not the quiet docile individual his brother might remember from his youth. On the contrary, he had become the ultimate Jewish warrior. Living the 613, and living them with a fire. This is the forward movement of the Vilna Gaon.

In a witty variation of this growth progression, the late YU *rosh yeshiva* Rav Yerucham Gorelic would say that we may all be on the A Train (the train that one would take to go from Manhattan to Yeshiva University) but it makes a difference whether we're heading uptown or downtown. You can face uptown, but if that's not the way your train is moving, then you're not going to get there.[173]

---

173 Oral discussion with my teacher Rav Herschel Schachter.

Infinite Light

We have looked at three perspectives on time: Rebbe Nachman says life is like a dreidel, Maharal presents the spiral view of Jewish history, and the Vilna Gaon postulates that either we're moving up or we're moving down. Let us take these three concepts a step further.

In Kabbalah we have a concept called *ohr ein sof* – the infinite light. How are we to understand this primordial infinite light? Spiritualist Rabbi David Aaron shares an analogy that strikingly clarifies this esoteric concept. Imagine that you are walking into a magic store. In the corner of this magic store they sell flashlights that are assembled with all different types of lights. You could, for example, buy the anatomy flashlight. When you shine this flashlight on your hand you don't see a hand, but rather you see bones, muscles, ligaments, etc. Or you could buy the art flashlight, and when you shine this flashlight on your hand you see your hand like a Picasso. There are hundreds of possible flashlights for you to try. But then you get to the *ein sof* flashlight. You pick it up with curiosity and shine it on your hand. Suddenly you see, for the first time, your true self.[174]

This is how the mystics have related to the light of Chanukah. Of the Chanukah candles we say, "*Assur l'hishtamesh bahem ela lirosam bilvad*" (it's forbidden to use them except to look at them). What does that mean? The whole year we don't benefit directly from the light source. Rather, we derive benefit from its byproduct, which is the light. When we walk into a room we can use the room for its true function because it is lit, but we pay little attention to the light itself. On the Sabbath the candles we light are lit because more light in the home brings greater peace in the home. That is also benefiting from the byproduct of light. However, on Chanukah it is the light source itself which must be enjoyed, not its byproduct. Why? Because like the infinite light, it is the truest vision of this world. It's the closest we can come to perceiving the Infinite One.

---

174 David Aaron, "Chanukah: The Light of Love," *Rabbi David Aaron*, http://www. rabbidavidaaron.com/chanukah-the-light-of-love/#more-2069 (accessed February 3, 2014). Used by permission.

This deepens Rebbe Nachman's "life is like a dreidel" concept. On Chanukah we look into the flame and in there we can pay witness to the True Source. It is with this conception that we understand that the dreidel is not spinning randomly; rather, it is being guided. While some of us live a lot of our lives on *shin* and many on *heh*, when you take a step back from the dreidel tournament and acknowledge that G-d is controlling the dreidel, you realize everything is there for a reason. I can begin to understand why I need that *nun* right now in my life. It's not random.

We began to develop the Maharal's concept of Jewish time working like a spiral, in which we visit the same spiritual points each year but on a different plane. According to the Gemara, one of the decrees of the Greek government against the religious Jews was that they were no longer welcome to bring their *bikkurim* (first fruits) to the Temple. Why not? According to the Mishnah, one had until Chanukah to bring one's first fruits to the Temple. Chanukah is a perfect marker because it symbolizes renewal. Chanukah symbolizes a people's ability to rise up and renew their mission. Rebbe Nachman of Breslov says that Yavan (Greece) has the same numerical value as *galgal* (wheel), because their relationship to time is determinant, fatalistic, and cyclical. Maharal's understanding of the Jewish calendar is a constantly progressing spiral that allows us to revisit the same point and renew it.

Let us look again at the Vilna Gaon's notion of progress and growth. When open miracles rear their heads in our faith, they always appear for a specific reason. We don't receive miracles for their own sake. Chanukah classically celebrates the emergence of a *pach katan* – one small jug of oil. Leaving aside the question of why we needed the miracle to begin with (when in fact *tumah hutrah b'tzibbur*, impure items are permissible in the public sphere[175]), why did the miracle manifest via one small jug as opposed to the miraculous finding of a whole barrel of oil?

The *Sefas Emes* posits that the Jewish people were at that moment at a very low spiritual spot. They didn't have much in the religious tank.

---

175 Babylonian Talmud, *Yoma* 8a.

Hellenism had made significant inroads into the Jewish community and psyche. The significance of this "small" miracle was to illustrate that in order to achieve victory in our lives we don't need to have a perfect past, we don't need to be Yosef Hatzaddik, all we need is that one little jug – call it the *pintele Yid,* the kabbalistic *nitzoz* (spark), or the jar of heart. Rav Tzvi Meir Zilberberg says that this idea conforms with the position of Beis Hillel with regard to lighting on Chanukah. The ideal is that we light by adding one more candle each night – *mussaf v'holech* (adding and moving forward). All we need to elevate ourselves is to start small, and from there we can conquer an army.

ALL THE WATER IN THE WORLD –
LAG B'OMER AND SHAVUOS

The middle of the Omer is a time of tremendous *din* (judgment). This time period marks the loss of Rebbi Akiva's twenty-four thousand students. How can we dance on Lag b'Omer, right in the middle of this dark season? Lag b'Omer centers around our celebration of Rebbe Shimon bar Yochai. Who is Rebbe Shimon bar Yochai that we celebrate his life almost more than any other religious figure?

There is a powerful verse in Song of Songs (8:7): "*Mayim rabbim lo yochlu l'chavos es ha'ahavah*" (abundant waters cannot put out the love) between G-d and His people.

When there is love, no storm, no hail, no earthquake can break our ability to stand. Love is a funny thing. It lends us a spirit that is so powerful.

There is a tradition that we stay up on Shavuos night and learn Torah throughout the night. What is the purpose of this custom? If our intention is to celebrate receiving the Torah by learning more Torah, then wouldn't it make more sense if we got a good night's sleep and learned the entire day from sunrise until midnight? Instead, we have thousands of people learning half asleep and for a shorter period of time. Why?

When I was in high school at YULA, my *rosh yeshiva* was Rav Shalom Tendler. He told the students the following anecdote. He was dating his soon-to-be bride. Rav Shalom went over to his rebbe in the Mirrer Yeshiva of Brooklyn to ask him for dating advice. His rebbe asked him, "When are you seeing her next?" Rav Shalom answered that "she's taking a train in from Baltimore in the next few days." The rebbe told Rav Shalom, "Don't pick her up from the train station in New York." Rav Shalom answered, "But it's a snowstorm, why wouldn't I pick her up?" His rebbe answered, "That's exactly the point. Find out where the train stops halfway in between, and be there with flowers." Why? What's the message? To show somebody you care, you have to be willing to do something a little crazy. Staying up all night may not be the perfect strategy for making the most of every minute of learning, but it is a wild and crazy way to show G-d how abundant our love is. *Mayim rabbim lo yochlu l'chavos es ha'avaha.*

Lag b'Omer celebrates the life of Rav Shimon bar Yochai, Rashbi as he is called. Rashbi once said, "I can excuse every Jew from [divine] judgment (*Eruvin 65*)." How is he able to get all of us off the hook? Because Rashbi had the ability to see the amazing spark that is in each of us. He is able to see our flaws as part of a much bigger picture. This is like the Gerrer Rebbe's interpretation of the Mishnah in Ethics of the Fathers (1:6): "*V'hevei dan es kol ha'adam l'chaf zechus*" (we should judge *the entire person*). When we can look at a holistic view of each other, we can get past the tiny quirks.

The Mishnah in *Sanhedrin* 11 states that "*Kol Yisroel yesh lahem chelek la'olam haba*" (Every Jew has a portion in the world to come). Rav Tzadok Hacohen of Lublin once said on this Mishnah that the emphasis here is on "Kol Yisrael" – there is an entity called "all of Israel." When we are a group, when we are connected to each other, then we have a share in the world to come. When we can learn to love, then all the waters in the world cannot wash us away.

Why do we celebrate Lag b'Omer? Numerous attempts have been made to explain where our tradition regarding this day come from. The Talmud in *Yevamos* 62 which talks about the death of Rabbi Akiva's twenty-four thousand students (on account of whose deaths by plague we mourn during the Omer period) actually makes no mention of Lag b'Omer. According to the early commentator the Meiri, Lag b'Omer is the day on which Rabbi Akiva's students stopped dying. The problem with that approach is that it doesn't explain why we would celebrate; shouldn't the mourning actually begin then? An alternative and famous suggestion, stated notably by Rav Chaim Vital, is that Lag b'Omer is the day Rebbe Shimon bar Yochai passed away. This classic explanation is not mentioned in the earlier commentaries and therefore needs further exploration.

Perhaps we can synthesize the classic views and suggest a third reason for our Lag b'Omer celebrations. After losing twenty-four thousand students, Rabbi Akiva could have given up and said, "I can't bear to teach any longer." Instead he realized that now his charge was greater than ever. I *must* continue to teach. Rebbe Shimon bar Yochai was hunted down by the Roman government. While hiding in a cave with his son, he could have said, "What purpose is there left to my studies?" Instead, he began an unparalleled intense program of Torah study.

Lag b'Omer, then, is the festive story of the indomitable Jewish soul. It's the realization that every individual is an infinite world waiting to be discovered. And when those individual worlds learn how to love each other, nothing can stand in their way.

WHEN YOM YERUSHALAYIM MET SHAVUOS

There's a minor debate over which idiom came first: what does that have to do with "the price of tea in China" or "the price of eggs." The oldest known usage of a similar line in the Jewish world is the one made famous by Rashi when he quotes, "*Mah inyan Shemitah etzel Har Sinai?*" (Why is Shemitah placed next to Har Sinai?). Let us redirect this question and ask, "*Mah inyan Yom Yerushalayim etzel Har Sinai?*" or, "Why is Yom Yerushalayim right before Shavuos?" We may see their link as historical serendipity, or we can choose to see beyond the surface. Let us explore a possible understanding that can help to underscore the significance of the transition from Yom Yerushalayim to Shavuos.

There is no doubt that the central focus of Shavuos in its current iteration is *limmud Torah*, (Torah study). Beyond the specific reading of the Decalogue on the first day, and the sentiments of loyalty to *halachah* in Sefer Rus, many have a custom to spend the entire night studying Torah. This all-night marathon is a potential waste of time if we don't appreciate the profound gift that we were given with the Torah.

To understand a fraction of its significance, let us pose a question. According to the mystical sources, the world begins with *ohr ein sof*, a primordial infinite light. The entire world emanates from this initial light. Likewise, when humanity has completed its journey, the mystics teach us that the world will go back to a state of *ohr ein sof*. If the world starts in infinite light and ends in infinite light, what use can be this

151

lowly world in between? What's the point of this earthly existence if eventually everything is going to return to the state in which it began?

The great contemporary kabbalist and sage Rav Itcha Meir Morgenstern comments that this world allows for the emergence of Torah. When Torah manifests in the world, it allows the *ohr ein sof*, which will return at the end of time, to blaze with an even brighter and stronger power than it did before it came into the world. Torah brings a certain unique energy into the world that is totally transformational.

Moreover, the singular impact of Torah is unique in that it affects each of us differently. According to the first Lubavitcher Rebbe, in the Tanya (chapter 51, *Likutei Amarim*): "For the higher worlds receive this vitality and light in a somewhat more revealed form than do the lower; and all creatures therein receive the revealed aspect of vitality, albeit each according to its capacity and nature." Each of our natures is distinct. We vary at different levels as to the intensity by which we can receive a divine vitality. Allow your nature to be open to the most radiant light.

This is just a glimpse of the tremendous power of Torah. It is so powerful that it alters the nature of the untouchable *ohr ein sof* at the end of time. On the other hand it is strangely malleable, allowing each of us to relate to its energy at different levels. What is it about the Torah that can at one time be so potent, granting greater vibrancy to the *ohr ein sof*, and at the same time so diverse that it can be grasped on countless levels? I believe Yom Yerushalayim has the key to answer that question.

After Tisha b'Av we read seven haftorahs called the *shiva d'nechemta*, the seven consolations. According to the Chozeh of Lublin, each one of the *shiva d'nechemta* relates numerically to the lower seven kabbalistic *sefiros*. Therefore the haftorah of the first week is *chesed* (loving-kindness). The haftorah of the second week is *gevurah* (strength). The haftorah of the third week is *tiferes*, which is splendor, beauty, and symmetry. Now, in that third haftorah we read the fifty-fourth chapter of Isaiah. There is one verse in particular (12) that is quite challenging to translate. The prophet is talking about what Jerusalem will be like in the future: "*V'samti kadchod shimshosayich*" (I will make your windows [i.e., the walls of Jerusalem] of precious stones), "*v'sh'arayich l'avnei ekdach*, *v'chol gevulech l'avnei chefetz"* (and your gates will be precious stones and your borders desirous).

What does this mean? The Talmud in *Bava Basra* (75) asks, "What's *kadchod*?" Listen to the Talmud's explanation, which is that there is an argument between two angels in heaven over what stone this verse is referring to. This debate is waged in the celestial world between the angels Michael and Gabriel and in the present world between two brothers, Chizkiya and Rav Yehudah. One angel is of the opinion that the stone is the *shoham*, a translucent quartz, but the other angel says it is *yashpeh* or jasper, which is reddish brown. Hashem says that we should resolve this "*ka'din v'chadin*," like him and like him. That's *kadchod*.

In this highly esoteric exchange, G-d says that Jerusalem's reality will make way for the two stones. Both identities and colors will have a space in the character of Jerusalem.

The breastplate of the high priest had twelve stones. Each stone was connected to a different tribe. Rabbeinu Bachayei says that the *shoham* stone represented Joseph. The *yashpeh* stone was for Benjamin. *Shoham* spells Hashem and G-d was always with Joseph. It's also known that Joseph was spectacularly beautiful.

The red color of the *yashpeh* (jasper) represents *gevurah*, which is power and restraint. *Yashpeh* stands for *yesh peh*, meaning "there is a mouth." The Midrash tells us that during all the years that Joseph was missing Benjamin, Benjamin actually knew prophetically what had happened to Joseph, but he knew it was the will of G-d to not say anything so he restrained his thought.[176] *Gevurah* is the ability to hold back. Joseph is from the side of *chesed*. Benjamin is from the side of redness or power. The two angels arguing in heaven were Michael, who is water, and Gabriel, who is fire, the respective characters of Joseph and Benjamin.

Michael comes to tell Abraham he's having a child. Gabriel comes to destroy Sedom. Gabriel corresponds to Chizkya, from *chazak*, "be strong." Just as King Hezekiah came and restored some of the spiritual

---

176 *Tanchuma*, Vayeitzei 1.

grandeur of Jerusalem through his sweeping monotheistic reforms, his name also bespeaks the courage and power that it took to make it happen. Their opinion is that Jerusalem will be marked by power and *yirah* (fear). Michael and Rav Yehudah say that Jerusalem will be marked by beauty and grandeur, so in the end, Jerusalem is both.

Jerusalem is like Jacob with the attribution of *tiferes*, synthesis and harmony. Jerusalem or Yerushalayim comprises both qualities in its name. *Yeru* is *yirah* and *shalayim* is peace, equanimity. Jerusalem is a representation of the essential magnificence of Torah. On one hand, it is *gevurah*, so powerful that it can even bolster the *ohr ein sof*. On the other hand, it is so pleasant, so beautiful that it can create itself as meaningful and relevant to each one of us on our own levels.

The power of the Torah is that it exposes to us the possibility of *kedushah* in a bifurcated world. The perfect Torah was given to a complex people who will turn their hearts and their attention to a complex city. Jerusalem is a city of contradictions and dichotomy. The Torah teaches the *ohr ein sof* how to live in a different world than the one it once knew. So this is Yom Yerushalayim's connection to Shavuos. On Yom Yerushalayim we celebrate the city of two stones with two perspectives and two worlds. Dichotomy, fracture, and *machlokes* (arguments) are all part of the splendor of the Torah. The Torah is received on Shavuos. And from then on the *ohr ein sof* is changed…utterly.

Epigraph Permissions

Excerpt from *The Act of Creation*, by Arthur Koestler, © 1990 Arkana. All rights reserved. Used by permission.

Excerpt from *Philosophical Investigations*, 4th ed., by Ludwig Wittgenstein, ed. P. M. S. Hacker and Joachim Schulte, © 2009 John Wiley and Sons. All rights reserved. Used by permission.

Excerpt from Harold Kushner, *When All You've Ever Wanted Isn't Enough: The Search for a Life That Matters*, © 1986 Penguin. All rights reserved. Used by permission.

Excerpt from *Notebooks, 1942–1951*, by Albert Camus, © Centre Français d'exploitation du droit de Copie. All rights reserved. Used by permission.

Quote from Shaquille O'Neal cited in Steven Wine, "Heat 85, Pistons 82," March 2, 2007, © Associated Press. All rights reserved. Used by permission.

Quote from Tony Robbins, "Unleash the Power Within," © TR Corp. All rights reserved. Used by permission.

Quote from Antoine de Saint-Exupéry cited in Richard Rumbold, *The Winged Life: A Portrait of Antoine de Saint-Exupéry*, © 1952 Random House, David McKay Division. All rights reserved. Used by permission.

Excerpt from "Brighton Rock," written by Brian May, © 1974 Queen Music Ltd. Excerpt from "The Fallen Priest," written by Freddie Mercury, Mike Moran, and Tim Rice, © 1988 Mercury Songs Ltd. All rights administered by Sony/ATV Music Publishing LLC., 424 Church Street, Suite 1200, Nashville, TN 37219. All rights reserved. Used by permission.

Excerpt from "This Hard Land," by Bruce Springsteen, © 1998 Bruce Springsteen (ASCAP). Reprinted by permission. International copyright secured. All rights reserved.

Quote from Sandra Day O'Connor cited in *Sandra Day O'Connor: Justice in the Balance*, by Ann McFeatters, © 2005 University of New Mexico Press. All rights reserved. Used by permission.